Michael Heis



# Inflation Targeting and Financial Stability

## Monetary Policy Challenges for the Future

Springer

Michael Heise
Allianz SE
München, Bayern, Germany

ISBN 978-3-030-05077-1 ISBN 978-3-030-05078-8 (eBook)
https://doi.org/10.1007/978-3-030-05078-8

Library of Congress Control Number: 2019930073



This Springer imprint is published by the registered company Springer Nature Switzerland AG
The registered company address is: Gewerbestrasse 11, 6330 Cham, Switzerland

# Foreword

The great financial crisis was a crisis of trust. Faith in liberal capitalism to generate fair outcomes was shattered; confidence in political and economic elites to govern the system was broken. The widespread loss of trust has become the trigger point for the populistic movements around the globe that today dominate the political landscape.

One institution could escape the trust breakdown: central banks. This applies all the more so in Europe. The decisive monetary policy by the European Central Bank (ECB) not only averted financial Armageddon after Lehman but also saved the euro, Europe's single currency—and thus kept the European dream of a united but diversified Europe alive.

Trust is hard won but easily lost. The usefulness of ECB's policy measures has long passed its peak. That's the sobering conclusion of Michael Heise's new book which analyzes monetary policies since the great financial crisis, based on his work as Allianz's chief economist. This sounds like a dry exercise for experts. Far from it. Much more is at stake than just some technical questions of interest rate setting. Like it or not but the euro—and its underpinning monetary policy—is the touchstone of how Europe as a whole will succeed in defining its place in the twenty-first century. The euro is the key for sustaining Europe's position in a rapidly changing world.

That's why the actions of the guardian of the currency matter so much. Unfortunately, success breeds failure. The ECB's denial to exit from its ultra-expansionary and unconventional policies in due time creates severe risks for the future, not only for financial markets but for societies as a whole. Rising wealth inequality and lower retirement incomes of today's generation of savers are just some of the damaging side effects. Moreover, the ECB is now the largest investor in euro area government bonds—the line between monetary and fiscal policies becomes more and more blurred. How can the common currency meet the high expectations of European unity if based on monetary policy whose independence and credibility is compromised?

However, not all is lost. There is still time for a (accelerated) normalization of monetary policy. But that might not be enough, as Michael Heise argues in a convincing way. What is really needed is to adapt the intellectual foundations of monetary policy, namely inflation targeting, for the challenges of the future.

Michael Heise is no doomsayer. Quite the contrary. Although he does not turn a blind eye to the immenseness of the challenges we face, he charts a straightforward course toward facilitating more stable long-term growth through monetary policies. Repairing the modus operandi of the ECB is not a walk in the park. But it is of utmost importance. A bigger role of financial cycles in the conduct of monetary policies is one of the recommendations. With the buildup of large financial risks through continuously expansionary monetary policies, it will be so more difficult to build the European house. In that way, this book is an important contribution to the political debate on Europe. It's not a second too soon.

Allianz SE, München, Germany Oliver Bäte
October 2018

# Preface

The analyses and conclusions in this book are based on many years of research into monetary and financial developments at the Economic Research Department of Allianz SE. This research has also informed two master class lectures at Johann Wolfgang Goethe University in Frankfurt. I have benefited immensely from the comments offered by my colleagues at Allianz Research, discussions at the International Conference of Corporate Bank Economists, and the very able students at the University of Frankfurt. Many thanks also go to Theo Iberrakene, Lena Mueller, Benedikt Fritz, Lea Pirovino and Tim Schmalle who, as Allianz Research interns, helped with charts and research support. My colleague Katinka Barysch deserves special praise for an outstanding job in editing the text and giving clarity to many arguments. All remaining mistakes are my own.

The book is written from a business economist's point of view; it focuses on empirical relationships, not theoretical models. Although I refer to a wealth of research, I do not intend to offer a complete review of the extensive and detailed work that has been published in recent years. My aspiration is to cover the main lines of argument that are relevant for future monetary policy. I attempt to derive conclusions for monetary policy in a structured way, beginning with its impact on the economy and financial markets and showing its side effects and potential trade-offs. This leads me to the conclusion that the prevailing dogma of monetary policy, inflation targeting, should be modified and complemented with elements of financial market stabilization. Although the debate is not new, its relevance has grown enormously in recent years, as central banks around the world have stepped into uncharted territory with large-scale asset purchases and negative interest rates. Meanwhile, risks on financial markets are mounting once again. The individual chapters of the book have been designed as short essays that should allow readers interested in only certain issues to dive in and out. This aspiration necessitated some repetition, for which I may be forgiven.

München, Germany
November 2018

Michael Heise

# Contents

1 Introduction 1

2 Some Reflections on the Secular Decline in Interest Rates 5

3 Uncertainties About the Monetary Transmission Mechanism 31

4 Side Effects of Monetary Accommodation 51

5 Towards a Monetary Policy Fit for the Future 75

6 Conclusions 91

Appendix: Op-Ed List 95

# List of Abbreviations

| | |
|---|---|
| ABSPP | Asset-Backed Securities Purchase Program |
| APP | Asset Purchase Programme |
| BIS | Bank for International Settlements |
| BoJ | Bank of Japan |
| CBPP | Covered Bond Purchase Programme |
| ECB | European Central Bank |
| EU | European Union |
| EUR | Euro |
| ESRB | European Systemic Risk Board |
| Fed | Federal Reserve |
| GDP | Gross domestic product |
| HCPI | Harmonized Consumer Price Index |
| IMF | International Monetary Fund |
| IPO | Initial Public Offering |
| LTRO | Long-Term Refinancing Operations |
| OECD | Organisation for Economic Co-operation and Development |
| OMT | Outright Monetary Transactions |
| PSPP | Public Sector Purchase Programme |
| QE | Quantitative easing |
| SMP | Securities Market Programme |
| TLTRO | Targeted Longer-Term Refinancing Operations |
| UK | United Kingdom |
| US | United States |
| USD | US Dollar |
| VAR | Vector autoregression |
| WWII | World War II |

# List of Figures


Fig. 2.1 The secular decline of interest rates in advanced economies 7
Fig. 2.2 Shifts in OECD age distribution 10
Fig. 2.3 Savings rates by geography 11
Fig. 2.4 Euro area: growing middle class and increased concentration of wealth 13
Fig. 2.5 Asset structure of wealth in the US, Western Europe and Japan 14
Fig. 2.6 Shifts in savings and investment curve 15
Fig. 2.7 Investment ratios in industrialized countries 15
Fig. 2.8 Where are global real interest rates heading in the long-term? 17
Fig. 2.9 Important ECB policy measures since 2008 20
Fig. 2.10 ECB balance sheet structure 21
Fig. 2.11 Germany: bond yields undershoot nominal GDP growth 22
Fig. 2.12 Ten-year euro-area bond yields and the term premium 25
Fig. 2.13 Estimated QE impact on 10-year German government bond yields (Mar 2015 to Jan 2018) 26
Fig. 3.1 Drastic liquidity injection without much effect in Japan 36
Fig. 3.2 Moderate increase of bank lending despite quantitative easing in the US 37
Fig. 3.3 Weak Eurozone bank lending despite balance sheet expansion by the ECB 37
Fig. 3.4 How valuation gains impact financial wealth 39
Fig. 3.5 House price index USA 40
Fig. 3.6 House price index Europe 41
Fig. 3.7 Balance sheet vulnerabilities 42
Fig. 3.8 Corporate bond holdings under asset management in the eurozone by rating 43
Fig. 3.9 ECB policy measures and the harmonized index of consumer prices 45

Fig. 4.1 Yields on financial assets and inflation in the eurozone 53
Fig. 4.2 Portfolio structure by income group 56
Fig. 4.3 Nominal total return by income group 57
Fig. 4.4 Cumulated changes in net interest income between 2008 and 2016 as percent of GDP 59
Fig. 4.5 Target II (im)balances rise to ever higher levels 60
Fig. 4.6 Inter-bank lending squeeze in the eurozone 61
Fig. 4.7 Fed policy and the cycle 64
Fig. 4.8 Deleveraging. What deleveraging? 67
Fig. 4.9 Overview of the main risks to financial stability in the EU 69
Fig. 5.1 Suggestion for an inflation indicator 79
Fig. 5.2 Global and regional FCIs and their components 82

# 1

# Introduction

Central banking has gone through a revolution since the financial crisis. The world's major central banks have amassed huge amounts of government debt and corporate securities, offered practically unlimited liquidity and lending opportunities for banks, pushed interest rates into negative territory and promised extremely low interest rates for some time to come. With such policies, central banks have broken various taboos, such as financing government deficits, negative interest rates or long-term loans to banks. But contrary to conventional wisdom, even these radical steps, which would have been unthinkable some years ago, have not yet triggered significant inflation.

For almost three decades, the prevailing dogma of central banking has been to target a certain rate of consumer price inflation. For several years following the financial crisis of 2008, however, inflation rates stubbornly diverged from central banks' targets. So central banks ventured into uncharted territory. Since 2017, inflation has begun to creep up again and central banks have started reducing their stimulus by slowly moving out of unconventional policies and, in the case of the US Federal Reserve and the Bank of England, also by raising interest rates. The European Central Bank (ECB) and the Bank of Japan (BoJ) however are still holding their central rates at zero and have not yet started reducing their balance sheets, which have grown tremendously in the course of quantitative easing with large scale asset purchase programs.

The impact of such unconventional monetary policies, especially central bank asset purchases, on growth and inflation are controversial. The significant and lasting deviations from central banks' targets opened a debate whether a narrow focus on inflation targets (or reference values) is the right concept for monetary policy. In order to draw such policy conclusions, it is important to


M. Heise, *Inflation Targeting and Financial Stability*,
https://doi.org/10.1007/978-3-030-05078-8_1

look at the various mechanisms by which monetary stimulus could feed into growth and inflation.

This book is organized as follows. Chapter 2 starts out by investigating the role of monetary policies in explaining the low yield environment that has characterized Western economies for many years. Obviously, the secular decline in nominal and real bond yields since the 1980s must have been influenced by some long-term fundamental factors affecting the global demand for and supply of capital; it cannot be explained only with reference to monetary policy. In recent years, however, central banks have exerted strong downward pressure on bond yields: first through forward guidance, which has strongly influenced interest rate expectations, and second through large bond purchase programs, which have reduced the risk premium embedded in bond yields.

Chapter 3 looks at the question whether the decline of bond yields has stimulated economic activity and, if so, how. Academic literature discusses many different monetary policy transmission mechanisms, which partly overlap: the credit channel, the bank channel, the portfolio channel, signaling effects and exchange rate effects. Their effectiveness is not beyond doubt and depends very strongly on prevailing macroeconomic conditions. Against the backdrop of an escalating financial crisis, central banks were forced to act decisively and quickly to prevent a downward tailspin of expectations and economic activity. Central banks had learnt this lesson from the Great Depression 90 years ago and they succeeded in halting the crisis.

In the years since 2008, however, the effects of monetary policy have been less clear. Economic demand did not seem to react much to interest rate changes. Inflation remained well below targets despite aggressive central bank action. These developments fueled a debate about secular stagnation or a "new normal" of low growth and low inflation.

The fact that the post-crisis recovery was so feeble in many countries can surely be attributed, in part, to weak supply and demand for credit. The credit channel of monetary transmission was more or less blocked, as banks, non-financial firms and households in many developed countries were de-risking and de-leveraging their balance sheets. In a "balance sheet recession", neither the level of interest rates nor the availability of liquidity are critical determinants of lending and borrowing decisions. The repair and stabilization of balance sheets takes priority.

Even monetary policy's positive impact on asset prices, which increased capital buffers and the value of collaterals did not generate a strong recovery of investment spending or consumer demand in the OECD's economies. The acceleration of growth in developed economies in 2017 may have been strengthened by monetary policies, but other factors also drove growth, such as the recovery in many emerging markets, which led to a more synchronized development in the global economy, strong fiscal stimuli in the US as well as China, and continued balance sheet repair in Europe, combined with the lagged effects of structural reforms in some European economies.

Central banks remain confident about the positive impact of their policies. They argue that the recovery after the financial crisis would have been even weaker had they not pursued a radical policy stance. As this is a counterfactual statement—we do not know how the world's economies would have fared under a different policy scenario—economic models come into play. The ECB, for example, has repeatedly cited model calculations to show that its asset purchases considerably increased growth and inflation in the eurozone economy. These models, however, are themselves built on assumptions that can be challenged theoretically and empirically. One such assumption is a stable reaction of the output gap (the difference between potential GDP at full resource utilization and actual GDP) to interest rate changes, another is a positive relationship between inflation and capacity utilization (Phillips curve). Empirical data in recent years have thrown both assumptions into doubt.

Chapter 4 looks at some of the unintended side-effects of a long period of monetary accommodation. Low rates of return on a broad range of assets have significantly depressed interest income from savings, while private and public borrowers have benefited. Evidence also suggests that ultra-expansive monetary policies have exacerbated inequality, as higher-income earners have benefitted more from asset price increases than low-income earners, who tend to have few savings and usually store them in bank deposits that no longer yield interest. This effect, however, is more ambiguous once lower debt service costs and lower unemployment rates are taken into account. A more obvious effect of the prolonged period of low interest rates is that on financial stability. Low yields have driven investors to take more risk and positively affected asset valuations. The prices of bonds, equity and real estate all depend on the interest rate used for discounting the future income streams that these assets create. Rising interest rates can therefore trigger strong market corrections. They can also cause trouble for highly indebted governments that have become used to easy financing conditions or for economies with a highly leveraged private sector. As the International Monetary Fund (2018) puts it in its recent Global Financial Stability Report: "A more significant tightening in global financial conditions will expose financial vulnerabilities that have built over the years and will test the resilience of the global financial system. The ratio of total non-financial sector debt to GDP in jurisdictions with systemically important financial sectors stands at an all-time high of 250%, asset valuations remain stretched across several sectors and regions, and underwriting standards are deteriorating, including in many segments of market-based finance."

These concerns are making it difficult for central banks to exit from expansionary policies. The US Fed has taken the lead with a very gradual course of normalization, slowly raising interest rates since the first hike in December 2015. The Fed's solid guidance on its gradual approach as well as a strong US economy have prevented harsh market reactions—with the exception of the taper tantrum in 2015.

The ECB and the BoJ have been much slower in reducing the degree of accommodation. With this, they may have avoided potential adjustment costs in their respective economies. Their stance, however, leaves them badly prepared for the next downturn or recession. With interest rates still very low, they may be forced to fight the next slowdown through further quantitative easing (QE) and even bigger asset purchases. QE would then become the "new normal" and monetary financing of governments might not be far away, as discussed in Chap. 5.

The main recommendation offered in this book is to allow more room for financial stability considerations and more discretionary elements in monetary policy decisions, rather than to stick to narrow, seemingly simple rules, such as a strict inflation target. There are many circumstances when central banks will be justified in allowing a temporary undershooting or overshooting of inflation, especially if there are risks (or trade-offs) with respect to financial stability or growth. Even in the longer run, inflation targeting hits its limits in an increasingly globalized and digitized world, where price competition is becoming more intense, wage increases remain moderate even in economies close to full employment and big swings of commodity prices affect overall price levels. Such international influences may at times dominate the domestic drivers of inflation—the only ones which the central bank can hope to influence.

## Reference

International Monetary Fund (2018) Global financial stability report, October 2018: a decade after the global financial crisis: Are we safer?

# 2

# Some Reflections on the Secular Decline in Interest Rates

*Understanding why interest rates have fallen is essential for both monetary policy and financial stability.*
Ferrero et al. (2017, p. 1)

**Abstract** The chapter investigates to what extent the decade long decline in bond yields has been the result of long-term economic trends and to what extent it has been caused by expansionary monetary policies. Central banks have pointed to a number of long-term trends behind the secular decline of bond yields that has been observed in many developed markets since the early 1980s. Among the most important such trends are demographic shifts, which have influenced savings patterns, and declining productivity growth rates, which dampened rates of return. While these and other fundamental factors certainly play an important role in explaining the low yield phenomenon, monetary policy measures since the crisis have also had a significant impact on bond yields—an impact that has been stronger than most forecasters had expected.

## 2.1 Fundamental Factors

The low level of interest rates has been a subject of contentious debate in recent years. Central banks have received much of the blame, particularly in countries with high savings rates. Many people suspected an act of "financial


M. Heise, *Inflation Targeting and Financial Stability*,
https://doi.org/10.1007/978-3-030-05078-8_2

repression", a planned redistribution of income from savers to debtors in the private sector, but most of all to the government. True, governments have benefited on a grand scale as low interest rates have reduced debt servicing costs and eased borrowing constraints. For savers, meanwhile, low interest rates have been like an invisible tax that reduces the growth of financial assets.

Central bankers and economists, however, have been offering an alternative explanation, one that looks more at fundamental changes in the economy. An important hypothesis is that in our aging societies income earners save with a view to retirement even at very low interest rates. Their time preference for consumption seems to have changed, saving today for future consumption has become more important. The decline in productivity growth rates and depressed capital demand by corporate investors are said to have exacerbated the decline of yields (Fig. 2.1).

A large amount of research looks at the drivers of the secular decline of bond yields. Still, it is not fully conclusive, and the effects are difficult to quantify.[1] According to former Fed chairman Ben Bernanke, the decline of yields reflects an increase in global capital supply, a "savings glut" created by high saving rates in industrialized countries as well as emerging markets in recent decades. While the large savings pool in industrialized countries reflects the growing need for retirement assets in aging societies, the capital exports of emerging markets are linked to an economic model that prioritizes exports over domestic consumption. Meanwhile, on the demand side, investment demand has been rather weak across the OECD. One reason may have been weak population growth, which translates into moderate long-term growth expectations. Rising political and economic uncertainties may also have affected the propensity to invest. Another reason may have been the declining relative prices of capital goods as investment shifts to intangible assets due to technological innovation.

It is difficult to calculate the contribution of these various factors to the secular decline of interest rates. One approach is to investigate whether the trends in the global supply and demand for capital are co-integrated with the trend in interest rates. This can be done in a non-formal manner or by using econometric models. Another strand of the literature tries to find an explana-

[1] References for this chapter include: Rachel and Smith (2015), Ferrero et al. (2017), Holston et al. (2016), Heise et al. (2016), Borio et al. (2017), Bernanke (2013), Deutsche Bundesbank (2017) and Laubach and Williams (2001).

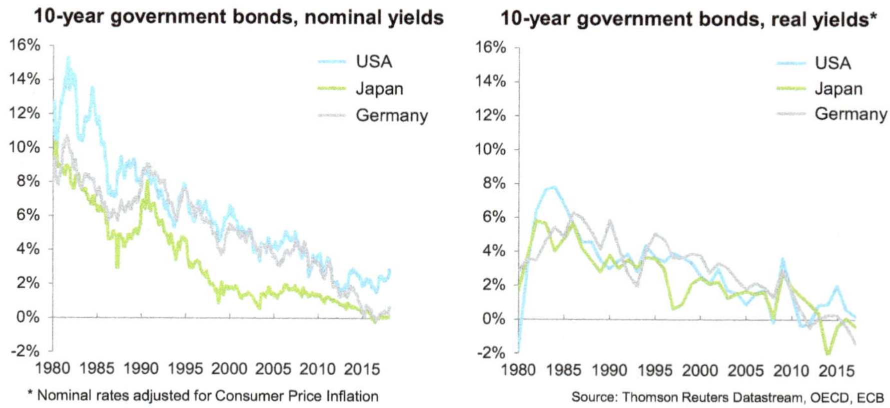


**Fig. 2.1** The secular decline of interest rates in advanced economies

tion by calculating an unobserved equilibrium or natural (real) rate of interest with macroeconomic models, the so-called r*. The equilibrium rate of interest keeps the economy fully utilized at a stable rate of inflation. The basic structure of these models makes the output gap (Y − Y*), with Y* as potential output a function of the difference between the real interest rate (r) and the equilibrium rate (r*).

$$Y - Y^* = \alpha\,(r - r^*)$$

The second main relationship is that the change in the rate of inflation (π) depends on the output gap.

$$\pi - \pi_{-1} = \beta\,(Y - Y^*)$$

In this model an increase in the rate of inflation implies that the market interest rate is below the natural rate. Falling inflation indicates the reverse. Most studies show that this equilibrium rate has declined since the great financial crisis. But estimates by how much vary widely depending on model specification and estimation technique: A 95% confidence interval puts them somewhere between −4 and +4% for the US and Germany, as shown in the 2016/2017 report by the German Council of Economic Experts.[2] Research by the Bank for International Settlements (BIS) also casts some doubt on the

[2] German Council of Economic Experts (2016, p. 205), see also German Council of Economic Experts (2017, Chap. 4).

view that the decline of bond yields has been mainly caused by non-monetary factors determining the demand and supply of capital. “Overall, our results raise questions about the prevailing paradigm of real interest rate determination. The saving-investment framework may not serve as a reliable guide for understanding real interest rate developments. And inflation may not be a sufficiently reliable signal of where real interest rates are relative to some unobserved natural level. Monetary policy, and financial factors more generally, may have an important bearing on persistent movements in real interest rates.”[3]

The big difficulties in robustly calculating the equilibrium real interest rate—and for that matter also potential output—call into question the usefulness of this concept for monetary policy making. Taylor and Wieland[4] argue estimates of time varying real equilibrium interest rates are not yet useful for application to current monetary policy, as different simulation techniques can radically change the results. Jay Powell,[5] in his recent Jackson Hole speech, also gives a vivid analysis of the difficulties guiding monetary policy decisions by model-based estimates of unobservable variables like r* and Y*.

To form an opinion on the fundamental factors behind the long-run interest rate decline, we need to look at some basic trends. The first observation is that we have seen not only a long-term decline in nominal bond yields but also, to a somewhat lesser extent, in inflation-adjusted real yields. As suggested by standard interest rate theory, the Fisher equation, the reduction in nominal yields reflects the disinflationary trend that the world experienced since the high inflation of the 1960s and 1970s. In the early 1980s, the Fed under Paul Volcker made sure that inflation and inflationary expectations did not get entrenched. Other countries were fighting inflation as well—first using quantitative targets for monetary growth, later targets for consumer price inflation. These policies successfully lowered the rate of price level increases, but only at the cost of rather significant output and job losses.

---

[3] Borio et al. (2017 p. 2); Rachel and Smith (2015) see a bigger role for fundamental factors: “Long-term real interest rates across the world have fallen by about 450 basis points over the past 30 years. The co-movement in rates across both advanced and emerging economies suggests a common driver: the global neutral real rate may have fallen. Although there is huge uncertainty, under plausible assumptions we think we can account for around 400 basis points of the 450 basis points fall. We think the global saving schedule has shifted out in recent decades due to demographic forces, higher inequality and to a lesser extent the glut of precautionary saving by emerging markets. Meanwhile, desired levels of investment have fallen as a result of the falling relative price of capital, lower public investment, and due to an increase in the spread between risk-free and actual interest rates.”

[4] Taylor and Wieland (2016) and Michaelis and Wieland (2017).

[5] Powell (2018).

Since the late 1980s, further disinflationary factors came into play, particularly the emergence of new competitors in Asian emerging markets and later in the former communist countries. Intensifying global competition in goods markets limited the potential for wage increases in developed countries. Later, the start of the digital revolution reinforced this trend by creating further price competition. These factors go a long way in explaining the decline of inflation and of nominal bond yields. They do not, however, explain the observed decline of real yields, calculated as the difference between nominal yields and consumer price inflation.

To find the driving factors behind the decline of real bond yields, it is important to note that sovereign bond yields have followed a similar downward trend across countries. The significant degree of market integration suggests that global drivers of supply and demand for capital have been at work. Specific national savings and investment trends are not irrelevant, especially when they influence risk spreads of a country, but global factors will prove dominant. In integrated global markets capital will flow to those countries where the rates of return are high. Therefore, over time, there should be a tendency of equalization of real bond yields as well.

Several long-term trends may have affected the global supply of capital. First, the **pattern of demographic change** matters. In past decades, most western industrialized economies have experienced both population growth and employment increases. Active workers typically have higher savings rates than retirees. Hence the volume of savings in many OECD countries has been substantial. However, once the strong age cohorts (baby boomers) in developed countries retire and the share of elderly people rises, overall household savings will decrease. This process has already started as Fig. 2.2 shows. While the share of economically active people will decline in coming decades, that of people over 60 will rise strongly. Older people do not save as much and often consume more than they earn by drawing down their savings in the process (dissaving).

It is entirely predictably that these demographic shifts will put strong pressure on pay-as-you-go pensions systems. Hence, today's workers must make stronger efforts to build up their own retirement savings. Low interest rates compound the problem, as they are slowing down the prospective growth of financial wealth. The continuing decline of trend productivity growth has further added to the propensity to save: When households adjust their expectations of future income because of low productivity growth, they tend to save more in an attempt to smooth their consumption patterns over the life cycle. All these factors help to explain why savings rates have been remarkably stable

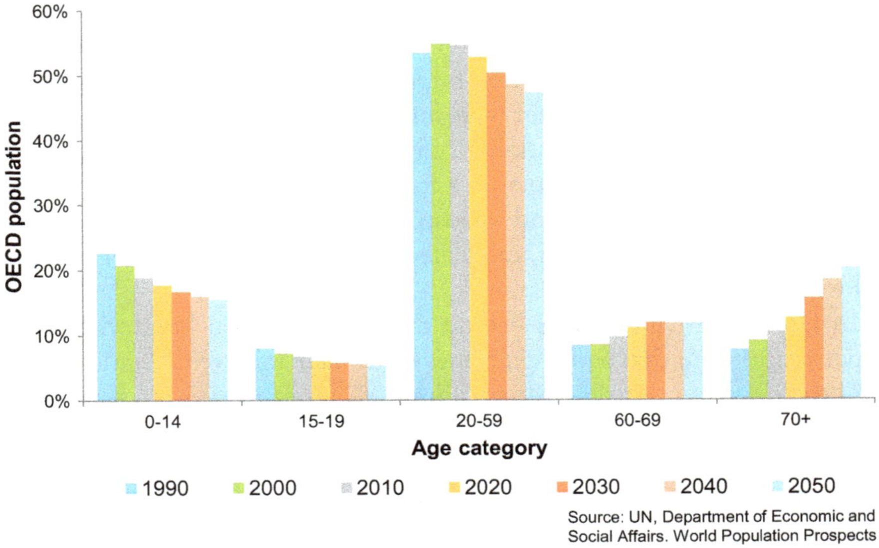


**Fig. 2.2** Shifts in OECD age distribution

in the EU and the US despite the massive decline in interest rates, especially since the financial crisis (Fig. 2.3).[6]

Japan has been the only large country with a secular decline in the savings rate. Here population growth has been slowing since the mid-1970s, and the aging of the society set in earlier and more forcefully than in other countries. The growing number of elderly Japanese have on average lower savings rates than active workers and partly even draw down their wealth.[7] Japan serves as a reminder for other countries that the demographic effect on savings is likely to change in the next decades. As baby boomers retire and the society ages, the overall savings rate is bound to decline. The retirement of baby boomers will accelerate in the EU and the US in the years after 2020.

Higher savings are often seen as a result of **increasing inequality** in the distribution of wealth and income. Rich people tend to save a higher share of their income than poorer ones. Hence, if there is redistribution to the benefit of the wealthy the average saving ratio will rise and interest rates may go

[6] A strong impact of demographic change is also calculated by Ferrero et al. (2017, p. 8). They cite further literature showing the importance of demographic factors for savings aggregates.

[7] Interestingly, the real interest rates have not been systematically lower in Japan than in the US or the EU, as deflation prevailed for many years.

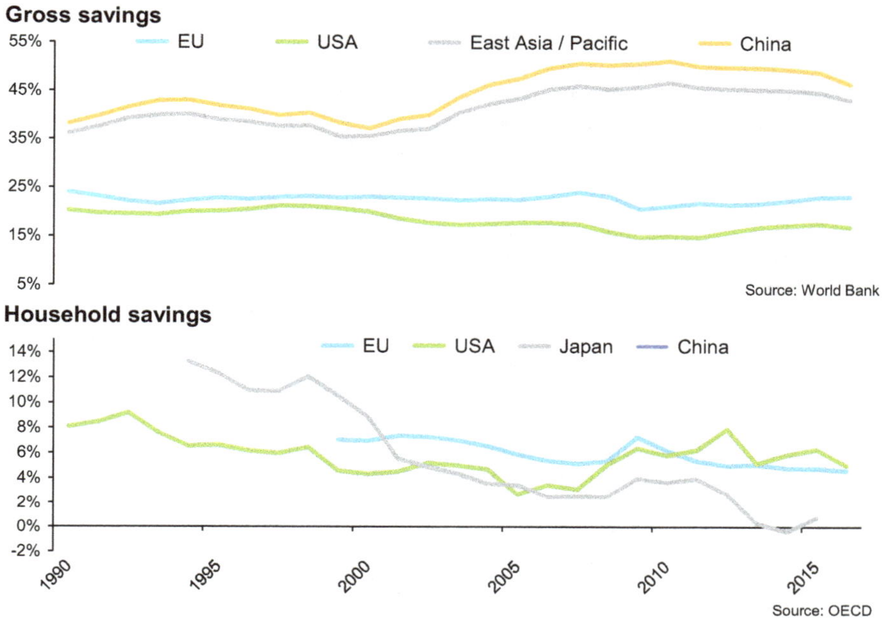


**Fig. 2.3** Savings rates by geography

down. Although this sounds plausible, the effects are more complex. First, there is no clear trend regarding inequality in industrialized countries. While the US has seen rising inequality for decades and also in the aftermath of the financial crisis, it has been falling in other countries' income and wealth distributions.

**The development of inequality** has many dimensions, national and international, concerning wealth and income, and before and after redistributive measures of governments. Looking at changes in the distribution of financial wealth in euro member countries in recent years, the data does not confirm generally rising inequality and the often cited compression of the middle wealth class. An Allianz (2016a) study splits all households/individuals in the euro area into wealth classes, based on net per capita financial assets in the eurozone. Applying international conventions, the euro middle wealth class encompasses all individuals with assets between 30 and 180% of the average value. The low and high wealth classes are defined accordingly. Net wealth includes all financial assets and household debt, but does not include real estate. In 2015, net per capita financial assets in the euro area amounted to an average of EUR 47,800—up by more than 50% since the beginning of the monetary union. That is a significant increase but still clearly lower than that of global wealth which doubled in the same period. In the US—where the economy also had to weather severe financial storms—assets have increased by more than 80% since 2000. The slower growth of net financial assets in the euro area comes as little surprise given that growth rates have been lagging behind the global average. What does come as a surprise, however, is that out of the three euro area wealth classes, only the middle class saw its membership swell (Fig. 2.4). The two other wealth classes—particularly the high wealth class—contracted in terms of their share of both the population as a whole and net financial assets. This trend does not support the theory that wealth inequality is on the rise in the euro area. Quite the opposite: the middle class is growing! This overall trend, however, masks substantive differences between individual countries. While the distribution of wealth has become more equal in Belgium, Germany and the Netherlands, this does not apply to Greece, Ireland and Italy, where there has even been a marked deterioration in equality. The crisis has left lasting scars in Greece in particular: whereas around half of the Greek population were members of the middle wealth class when the euro was launched, the figure stood at only 20% in 2015. And there is another aspect that deserves attention. Although the share of net financial assets in the hands of the euro high wealth class is getting smaller, this does not apply to the richest population decile. This group's share of total wealth has been growing continuously ever since the euro was introduced. As a consequence, wealth is now more concentrated in the hands of the upper decile.

In conclusion, changes of wealth distribution within the euro area are not clear cut. The evidence does not seem to confirm the fears of an erosion of the middle class and associated concerns about social exclusion, at least for the euro area as a whole (although the fears certainly hold true for Greece). At the same time, however, wealth would appear to be increasingly concentrated in the hands of a small elite: the rich are becoming richer and distancing themselves further and further from the average.

The relationship between inequality, savings and the real interest rate is further complicated by a possible impact of inequality on growth. If inequality dampens growth then it will also dampen interest rates. For the US, this seems to be the common assumption: inequality is seen as a brake on growth through less consumption, possibly also less productivity and less attainment of skills. But this need not be the case in other countries which have a more equal income distribution. Inequality can provide incentives for workers to upgrade their qualification or to invest more in their career, thereby fostering growth. Thus, higher growth would imply higher, not lower interest rates. Therefore, it seems near impossible to attach a number to the impact of inequality on savings and interest rates.

Apart from changes in the volume of savings, the return on safe assets such as benchmark government bonds or safe bank deposits will also depend on

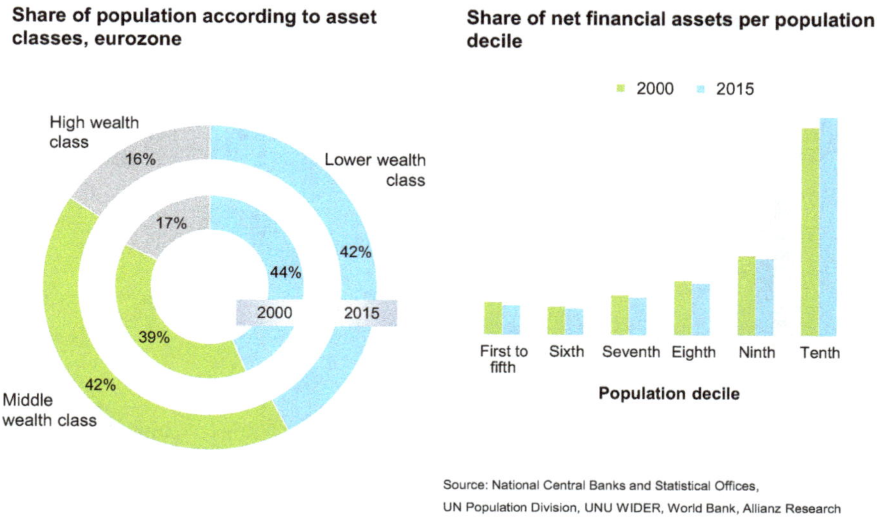


**Fig. 2.4** Euro area: growing middle class and increased concentration of wealth

the **investment preferences of savers**. In recent years, savers have preferred safety and liquidity, after two big financial crises in one decade—the dot.com and the subprime bubble—wiped out large amounts of private wealth. In Western Europe, the equity shares in household portfolios have remained rather low. Some 30% of gross financial wealth is invested in bank deposits and about 40% in life insurance policies and pension vehicles. Life insurers and pension providers invest heavily in safe bonds, as they operate under strict rules that force them to hold sufficient capital to back the guarantees and promises they have made. In the US more money is invested in securities and the equity ratio is higher than in Europe. But, here the combined share of bank deposits and insurance and pensions is around 45%, too (Fig. 2.5).[8]

Finally, global savings volumes have been pushed up by remarkably strong income growth and **high savings ratios in emerging markets**. The high pace of savings growth in these countries was not fully absorbed by domestic investment activity. Consequently, the surplus of savings was exported to world capital markets, a development which was branded as the savings glut by former Fed Chairman Ben Bernanke. Figure 2.3 shows the high level of total gross savings in Asian Emerging markets, including household, corporate and public savings. As gross savings exceeded gross investment, large current

[8] Allianz (2017).

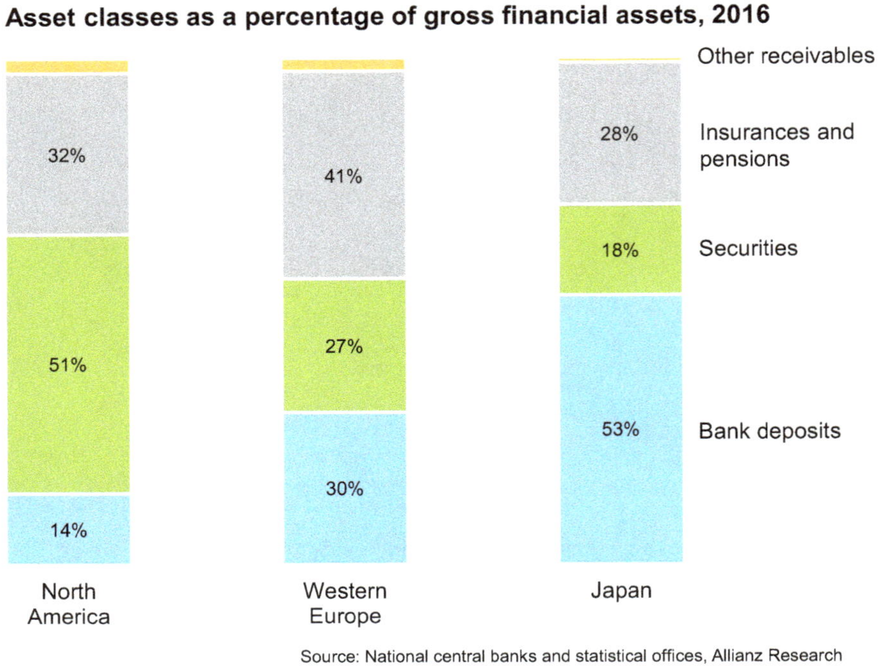


**Fig. 2.5** Asset structure of wealth in the US, Western Europe and Japan

account surpluses developed in China and other Asian economies. Together with the surpluses in the oil exporting Gulf States, this group of emerging markets therefore also contributed strongly to the global savings glut.

**Illustrative shift in the supply and demand for capital.** While there are many good reasons for a global rise of savings in past decades, they do not give a full explanation of the real interest rate trends observed. If there had been only an increase in global savings, then we would have seen not only a decrease of bond yields, but also a rise in investment ratios. This suggests that there has also been a downward shift in global investment demand, a reduction of investment at any given rate of interest. Additional savings plans were not met by additional investment plans, therefore the interest rate had to decline quite significantly to generate a new equilibrium on global capital markets. Simplified in a stylized graph, the global savings function, relating the savings volume to the real interest rate, has shifted to the right from $S_0$ to $S_1$, whereas investment demand shifted to the left from $I_0$ to $I_1$. The result has been a strong decline of real bond yields to $r_1$ without necessarily generating an increase in investment and savings (Fig. 2.6).

For the last two and a half decades, **investment demand as a share of GDP** has been relatively stable or even declined slightly in larger advanced

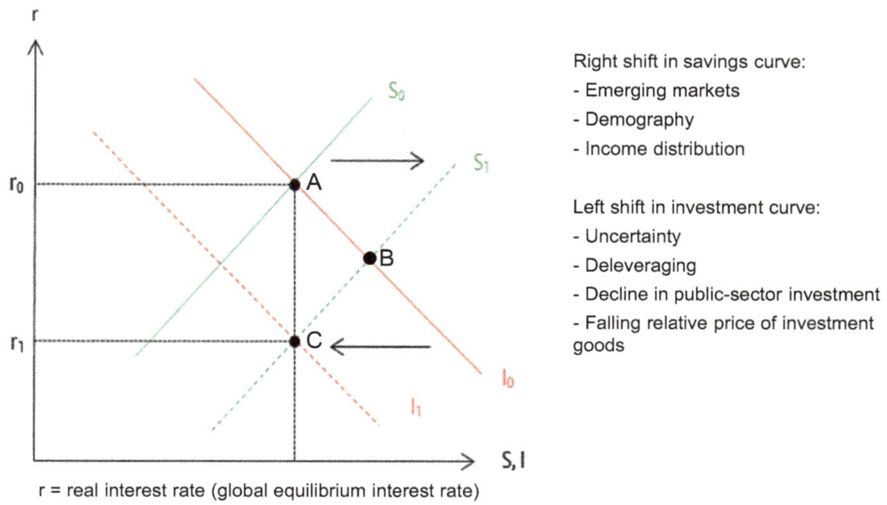


**Fig. 2.6** Shifts in savings and investment curve

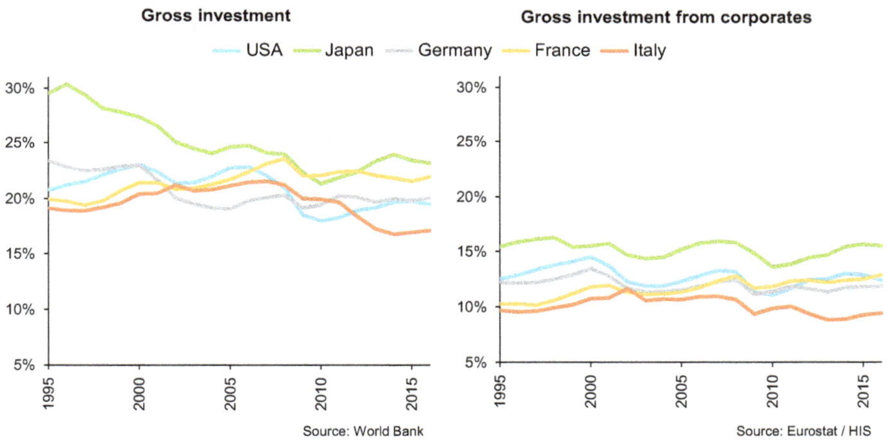


**Fig. 2.7** Investment ratios in industrialized countries

economies (Fig. 2.7). In some countries weakening public investment played a role. Corporate investment ratios were more stable, but they did not increase in a way one might have expected as a result of the strong downward trend in interest rates. Corporate investment proved to be quite interest inelastic and it took many years for it to reach the pre-crisis levels despite falling interest rates. Obviously, the financial crises, in particular the one in 2008/2009, damaged the investment climate as companies had to tackle huge impairments on assets, a mountain of bad loans and major uncertainties concerning the business outlook. So they reduced capital expenditure and hoarded cash, irrespective of how low interest fell. Technological changes may have also changed investment behavior. Intangible investments into software and digital platforms have become much more important. Investment activities have shifted away from traditional bricks and mortar. As the relative price of intangible capital goods declined with technological advances, so did the capex budgets of many companies.

Will real interest rates recover? The strongest argument for such a forecast would be the demographic change that is about to take place in the next decades in most western countries as well as many emerging economies, notably also in China, where the peak of the working population will be reached in the next years. Baby boomers in western countries will start to retire in big numbers in the coming years. They will not maintain their high savings rates. The number of people between 60 and 69 as well as over 70 will strongly increase in the OECD in the next decade and the ones following, as shown in Fig. 2.2. In many emerging markets, notably China, the negative impact of aging on savings volumes may be reinforced by changes in the economic growth model: from savings and over-investment to more consumption-driven growth. All in all the change is massive. While the world witnessed the largest ever positive labor supply shocks between the 1980s and the 2000s, resulting from demographic trends and the inclusion of China and Eastern Europe into the global economy, these trends are now reversing. That implies lower savings rates and a lower supply of capital in the future that should make real interest rates increase over time (Fig. 2.8).

But there are counter-effects, too. Unless productivity growth accelerates significantly, the reduction of the labor force will dampen growth, which, in turn, will dampen real interest rates. The Japanese experience is instructive. The aging of the Japanese society over past decades led to a reduction of the savings rate, but that did not push up real interest rates, as productivity growth and investment in the economy remained weak. In western developed countries more generally, real interest rates are unlikely to rise unless productivity growth and investment also increase.

Views on the future path of investment and productivity differ. In the near term, private investment looks set to rise, as the de-leveraging comes to an end and animal spirits return. But such cyclical forces will disappear if and when the financial markets and the real economy experience their next downturn. In the long run, and taking a more structural view, an upward shift of investment is by no means guaranteed as major uncertainties in the economic, technological and political environment are likely to persist. Weak demographics

| Driving factors | Impact on real interest rate: slightly up |
|---|---|
| Shift in saving curve<br>• Demography: rising proportion of older people<br>• Lower savings in emerging markets | Upward |
| Shift in investment curve<br>• Pressure from private sector deleveraging eases<br>• Public-sector investment rises slightly<br>• Importance of intangible investment remains high | Slightly upward |
| Portfolio shifts<br>• Little change of regulatory preference for government bonds<br>• Preference for safe assets on the side of investors remains? | Unchanged? |
| Productivity growth<br>• Positive impact of information and communication technology | Slightly upward |

**Fig. 2.8** Where are global real interest rates heading in the long-term?

themselves are a reason for companies not to follow overly optimistic growth and investment plans.

How about productivity growth and technological advances as a driver of higher interest rates? Productivity trends are notoriously difficult to forecast. Even an explanation of recent productivity trends is not easy: weak productivity growth in most developed countries seems to stand in stark contrast with the fast pace of technological change and the ongoing digitization of business. Many economists assume that the productivity effects of digitization will become more pronounced once new technologies have spread further, companies have transformed their business models and ways of working and labor markets have adjusted in line with new opportunities. But the jury is still out.

Another question that is relevant for bond yields concerns the impact of digitalization on the demand for capital. In recent years, there seems to have been little such impact. The relative price of capital goods has declined and investment has shifted from physical goods to intangible investments in software and digital platforms. This should reduce the demand for capital in the corporate sector. But there are other views, as expressed, for example, by Bain and Company, the management consultancy: "In the US, a new wave of investment in automation could stimulate as much as $8 trillion in incremental investments and abruptly lift interest rates. By the end of the 2020s, automation may eliminate 20–25% of current jobs, hitting middle to low-income workers the hardest. As investments peak and then decline—probably around the end of the 2020s to the start of the 2030s—anemic demand growth is likely to constrain economic expansion, and global interest rates may again test zero percent" (Bain and Company 2018). This quote shows the complexity of possibly changing dynamics of the developments in the future.

Our capacity to project the fundamental drivers of interest rates is modest at best. At present, the most plausible scenario is a moderate increase in real interest rates over the next 10 years. Fiscal and monetary authorities in most countries of the world have a strong motivation to keep interest rates from rising too strongly, as governments, and partly also the private sector, have piled up large amounts of debt. Significant interest rate rises would render servicing and rolling over that debt very difficult. Therefore, regulatory measures and monetary policies will continue to aim at low real rates for some time to come.

Returning to the quote at the beginning of this chapter, what can monetary policy actually learn from the analysis of the fundamental factors behind declining real and nominal interest rates over the decades? Different approaches and methods of analysis lead to diverging conclusions concerning the impact of fundamental factors on long-term interest rate trends.

It does not seem plausible that low bond yields during the years following the great financial crisis can be explained by fundamental factors driving down the "neutral" rate of interest. If this argument held true, it would follow that monetary policy has not actually been expansionary; it has merely followed a downward trend of underlying interest rates. Given that structural changes that impact global capital markets, such as demographics and productivity, work very slowly, this explanation is not sufficient. Rather it seems that monetary policies, especially in the eurozone, have pushed bond yields below their market equilibrium, as intended by the central bank. This is analyzed in the next chapter.

## 2.2 The Impact of Monetary Policy

In the years since the financial crisis of 2008, the impact of monetary policy on bond yields has been quite substantial. Central banks implemented various measures designed to reduce interest rates: virtually unlimited liquidity offered to banks, very low or even negative interest rates and substantial measures of quantitative easing. In many cases, the effects of individual measures were intended to reinforce each other. The ECB's announcement of quantitative easing, for example, also had an impact on the forward guidance on interest rates, as the bank had committed to first ending asset purchases before hiking interest rates.

The ECB's policy package (Fig. 2.9) involved a host of standard and non-standard tools of monetary policy.[9] Among the standard measures were multiple cuts in key interest rates. The interest rate charged for the main refinancing operations was reduced from 4.25% in September 2008 to 1.0% in May 2009. Faced with a seemingly quick recovery in 2010 and 2011 as well as rising inflation, the ECB raised its interest rates twice in 2011. It quickly reversed those hikes when the economy started slowing again and fears about a Greek sovereign default started to spook markets. In March 2016, the interest rate for the main refinancing operations reached zero.

Another immediate reaction of the ECB was to assume its lender of last resort function for the banking system. Given the financial structure of the euro area, where banks are the primary source of credit to the economy, the ECB adapted its existing monetary policy framework and provided liquidity to banks on a large scale. In 2008 it announced fixed rate full allotment tenders for banks to counter any liquidity shortages. A few months later, the ECB offered Long-Term Refinancing Operations (LTROs) that granted access to longer-term (1 year) liquidity at a predetermined rate in any quantity needed, provided the bank could offer adequate collateral. At a time when the interbank market was dysfunctional and spreads on this market skyrocketed, the ECB became an important source of funding for financial intermediaries. In the years following the financial crisis, the ECB's Governing Council frequently reviewed LTROs and extended their duration while broadening the range of acceptable collateral. In June 2014 the ECB took the important step to make these operations conditional on bank lending; they were renamed Targeted Longer-Term Refinancing Operations (TLTROs).

The Eurosystem of central banks started to employ the instrument of security purchases—('balance sheet policies') in 2009 with the first Covered Bond Purchase Program (CBPP1).The total aggregate value of this program was EUR 60 billion. In May 2010, the Eurosystem started the Securities Market Program (SMP), during which it bought securities worth EUR 230 billion. The second Covered Bond Purchase Program (CBPP2) was conducted between November 2011 and October 2012. In November 2014, national central banks started the Asset-Backed Securities Purchase Program (ABSPP). One month later, the third Covered Bonds Purchase Program (CBPP3) was

[9] A discussion of monetary policy instruments and objectives can be found in Draghi (2015), Draghi (2017) and Praet (2017).

| | ECB |
|---|---|
| 2008 | October: Fixed-rate tenders with full allotment (FRFA) as first operation under ‚Enhanced Credit Support'; extended list of eligible collateral for credit operations |
| 2009 | May: Announcement of first Long-term refinancing operations (LTROs) with maturity extended to 12 months to be conducted in June 2009<br>June: First Covered bond purchase programme (CBPP1) officially announced to begin in July 2009 |
| 2010 | May: Securities markets programme (SMP) to intervene in euro area public and private debt securities markets with operations to absorb the liquidity injected |
| 2011 | October: Second Covered bond purchase programme (CBPP2) announced to begin in November 2011<br>December: First Long-term refinancing operation with maturity of three years (LTRO1) announced and implemented |
| 2012 | February: Second Long-term refinancing operation with maturity of three years (LTRO2) announced and implemented<br>July: ‚Whatever it takes' by Draghi<br>August: Outright Monetary Transactions (OMT) to replace the SMP in sovereign bond purchases with no ex-ante limit |
| 2013 | July: Forward guidance concerning low interest rates for an "extended period of time." |
| 2014 | June: Marginal deposit rate drops to negative 10bp; first round of Targeted longer-term refinancing operations with maturity of 4 years (TLTRO I) to be conducted in September 2014<br>October: Announcement of Asset-Backed Securities Purchase Programme (ABSPP) and Third Corporate Bond Purchase Programme (CBPP3) under the APP |
| 2015 | January: Official implementation of the ‚Extended Asset Purchase Programme' (APP) with set amount of EUR 60 bn per month<br>March: Public Sector Purchase Programme (PSPP) under the APP |
| 2016 | March: Main refinancing rate hits zero lower bound and marginal deposit rate decreases to negative 40bp; second round of Targeted longer-term refinancing operations with maturity of 4 years (TLTRO II) announced to begin in June 2016<br>April: APP monthly pace increased to EUR 80 bn per month<br>June: Corporate Sector Purchase Programme (CSPP) under the APP announced and implemented<br>July: Key interest rates expected to remain low for extended period of time<br>December: APP monthly pace announced to decreased to EUR 60 bn per month, starting April 2017 |
| 2017 | October: APP monthly pace further decreased to EUR 30 bn per month, starting January 2018 |
| 2018 | May: Termination of APP still undetermined<br>July: Termination of the net asset purchases in 2019 |

Note: This table does not include the decisions of the Governing Council on rate changes and the prolongation or modifications of the liquidity operations that were taken in the Council meetings on various occasions.

**Fig. 2.9** Important ECB policy measures since 2008

introduced. One may also count the ECB's Outright Monetary Transactions (OMT) program among the non-standard measures, although no purchases ever took place under this crisis resolution program.

In January 2015, the Eurosystem then announced the Expanded Asset Purchase Program (APP) in an attempt to further loosen its monetary policy stance. The biggest part of the APP consisted of the Public Sector Purchase Program (PSPP) for bonds of central governments, agencies and European institutions, which complemented the other purchase programs of private-sector assets already under way. The ECB started PSPP purchases in March 2015, initially to the tune of EUR 60 billion per month. It raised the volume by EUR 20 billion in April 2016. Public sector securities accounted for more than 75%. In December 2016, the Eurosystem decided to reduce the monthly volume back to EUR 60 billion from April 2017 onwards. And in January 2018, the Governing Council reduced the size of monthly purchases further to EUR 30 billion. As a result of all these measures, the balance sheet of the ECB and the national central banks rose from 13% of GDP in 2006 to around 40% in 2017. By mid-2018, the ECB's balance sheet contained about EUR 2.3 trillion worth of bonds (Fig. 2.10).

How important have these interest rate and balance-sheet measures been for the development of long-term bond yields? A first indication of their

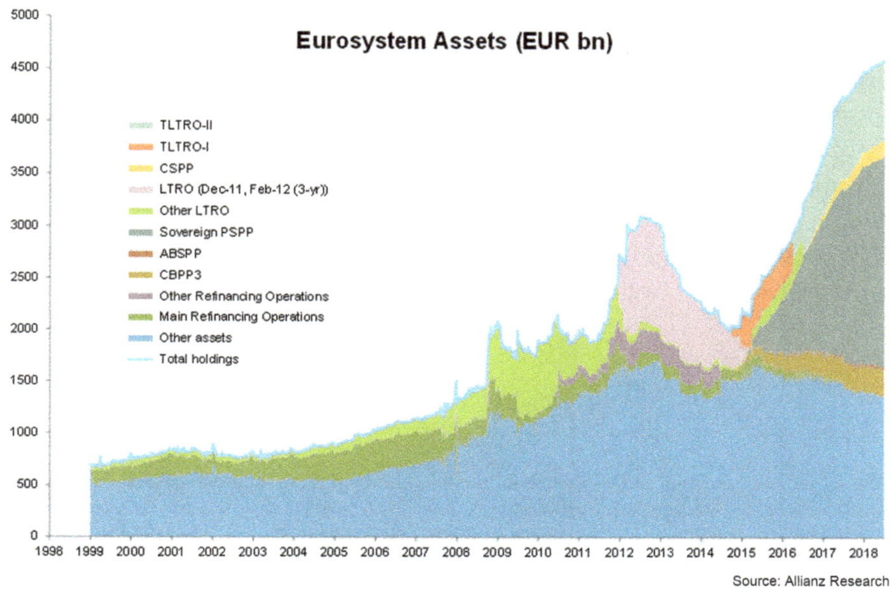


**Fig. 2.10** ECB balance sheet structure

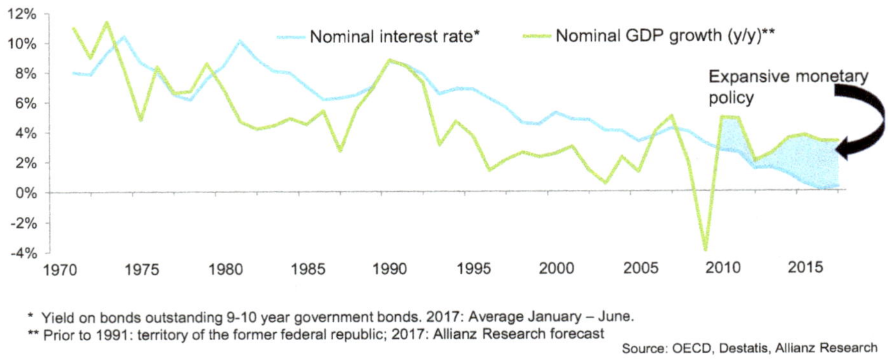


**Fig. 2.11** Germany: bond yields undershoot nominal GDP growth

importance is the fact that nominal bond yields have declined much more strongly than the growth rates of nominal GDP. As GDP growth reflects many of the aforementioned influences like weaker demographics, weaker productivity or low inflation, the undershooting of bond yields could be due to monetary policy.[10]

An instructive case study is the German sovereign debt market, the Bund market (Fig. 2.11). The German 10 year Bund yield has shown particularly strong deviations from the nominal GDP growth of the economy in recent years. Since 2008 the rate of return on these government bonds has moved towards the zero line, while GDP growth in the economy was rather solid. In former decades such deviations were limited to rather short periods of time (mostly in recessions). Most of the time, long-term Bund yields were clearly above the rate of GDP growth.[11]

The impact of monetary policy on bond yields can be dissected into two components: the expectation component and a term premium (see box). The ECB proved effective in keeping interest rate expectations low and reducing the term premium in long-term bonds. The forward guidance it gave on its

[10] The importance of nominal GDP-growth for nominal bond yields is not only an empirical observation, but can also be derived from neoclassical growth models. The logic is that, in a life cycle consumption model, a reduction of growth and income expectations leads to higher savings and lower market clearing interest rates. See, for instance, Rachel and Smith (2015, p. 11); Holston et al. (2016, p. 3); Council of Economic Advisors (2015, p. 14).

[11] The divergence between long-term bond yields and nominal GDP growth is especially pronounced for Germany, but it has—to a lesser degree—recently also been observable for the Eurozone as a whole.

own policy stance kept interest rate expectations low even in the years from 2016 to 2018, when economic growth accelerated and inflation normalized. When markets are convinced that the central bank will not hike rates for an extended period of time, this translated into lower bond yields. Over and above this expectations mechanism, central banks influenced bond yields through their large-scale purchases of sovereign or corporate bonds. These purchases influence the term premium, a risk premium for longer duration investments. By buying safe and longer duration bonds, the central bank added to the demand by banks, insurance companies, pension funds and other long-term investors that need long duration safe investments. This raises the prices for safe bonds and lowers the risk premia. The ECB was not deterred by high prices of bonds, rather its demand was price-inelastic as it stuck to the amounts set by the quantitative target for balance sheet expansion. A reduction of yields also through lower term premia was an intended effect of these policies.

These two mechanisms have been crucial for pushing bond yields below nominal growth in the euro area and many developed economies. Central banks were more powerful in this respect than many interest rate forecasters had expected. Bond yields have for years consistently been overestimated.

The calculation of the term premium is rather complex. It requires the use of term structure models that capture the interest rate expectations over long time horizons and calculate the price of a bond of certain maturity based on these forward looking expectations. If there is a divergence between this price

**Two major components of bond yields in a simple model.** Conceptually, observed bond yields can be broken down into a component that captures the expectations of future short-term interest rates (over the bond's lifetime) and a risk premium, or term premium. According to the market expectations hypothesis the shape of the yield curve for bonds depends on market participants' expectations of future short-term interest rates. For example, if investors have an expectation of what 1-year interest rates will be next year, the current 2-year interest rate can be calculated by compounding this year's 1-year interest rate by next year's expected 1-year interest rate. Interest rate expectations can be derived from future markets. So, more generally, returns (1+ yield) on a long-term instrument are assumed to equal the geometric mean of the expected returns on a series of short-term instruments:
Denoting $i_{st}$ and $i_{lt}$ as the expected short-term and actual long-term interest rates, this yields:

$$\left(1+i_{lt}\right)^{n}=\left(1+i_{st}^{year\,1}\right)\left(1+i_{st}^{year\,2}\right)\ldots\left(1+i_{st}^{year\,n}\right)$$

The above expectations model does not cover (interest rate and other) risks associated with holding longer-term assets as opposed to a sequence of shorter term investments. This is where the liquidity or term premium comes in. The underlying assumption is that long-term interest rates not only reflect investors' assumptions about future interest rates but also include a premium for holding long-term bonds. This premium compensates investors for the added risk of having their money tied up for a longer period. More precisely, it is the extra compensation they require for holding long-term assets over time rather than rolling over short-term exposures. The risks of holding longer-term bonds are primarily potential capital gains or losses that interest rate changes imply for long maturity investments. In addition, default risks rises with the length of the investment period. The risk premium can be added to the equation as follows:

$$\left(1+i_{lt}\right)^{n}=rp_{n}+\left(\left(1+i_{st}^{year\,1}\right)\left(1+i_{st}^{year\,2}\right)\ldots\left(1+i_{st}^{year\,n}\right)\right)$$

where $rp_n$ is the risk premium associated with an $n$ year bond.
Low or even negative term premia can occur for different reasons. If investors expect low interest rate volatility (reduced interest rate risk) or have high a demand for long-term safe assets (e.g. Treasuries or Bunds) in periods of financial stress, this will keep term premia low. Also, regulatory requirements for banks and insurance companies channel investments into long-term safe government assets. Finally, the asset purchase programs of central banks elevate the prices for long term bonds, as they are not motivated by risk or return considerations.

and the actual observed price this is the term premium. A number of studies in recent years have shown for both the US and European markets that during the years of QE a reduction in the term premium was a major reason for declining bond yields.[12] The launch of large scale purchase programs in combination with regulatory requirements for banks and institutional investors to improve capital buffers pushed yields below the value implied by interest rate expectations. Similar to other analyses, a study by the ECB comes to the conclusion that the decline in German government bond yields around the date of the announcement of the Public Asset Purchase Program in January 2015 was "…almost fully attributable to a decline in the term premium as opposed to the expectations component", Lemke and Werner (2017, p. 1).

Figure 2.12 shows calculations for the term premia in the US and the euro area for 10 year government bonds. These term premia have been low and mostly even negative since 2014. Negative term premia imply that investors are paying a price for holding long duration bonds and not receiving a risk premium to compensate for the higher risks.

[12] For example BIS (2017a), Lemke and Werner (2017) and Praet (2017).

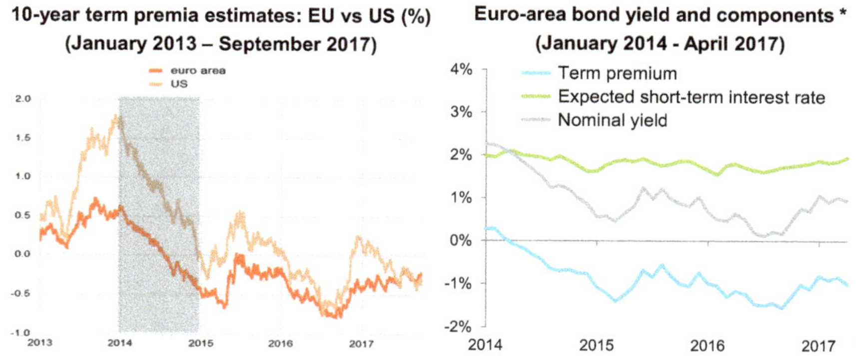


Notes: The US Treasury term premium is based on the term structure model by T. Adrien, R. Crump and E. Moench (2013), „Pricing the Term Structure with Linear Regression", *Journal of Financial Economics*, 110, pp.110-138; the euro area OIS term premium is based on the term structure model by Joslin, S., K. Singleton and H. Zhu (2011), „A New Perspective on Gaussian Dynamic Term Structure Models.", *Review of Financial Studies*, 24, pp. 926-970. The last estimates are for 29/09/2017.

Source: ECB, Benoît Cœuré: „Monetary policy, exchange rates and capital flows"

Notes : Decomposition of the 10-year nominal yield according to an estimated joint macroeconomic and term structure model; see P Hördahl and O Tristani, „Inflation risk premia in the euro area and the United States", *International Journal of Central Banking*, September 2014. Yields are expressed in zero coupon terms, for the euro area, French government bond data is used.

Source: Bank for International Settlements, Annual Report 2017

**Fig. 2.12** Ten-year euro-area bond yields and the term premium

A rough estimate of the impact of central bank asset purchases on bond yields can be derived from a standard regression equation for bond yields to which the amount of asset purchases is added as an independent variable, in addition to other explanatory factors, such as the yield of US Treasuries, short-term interest rates on eurozone and US markets and a dummy variable to catch the effect of the announcement of QE.[13] For the euro area this gives an impact of approximately −0.8 percentage points on the 10-year German Bund for the time when monthly asset purchases were at EUR 80 billion per month (Fig. 2.13). This figure includes the announcement effect that was visible in late 2015. This is a rough estimate, but it is in line with other analyses of a similar kind. The ECB also reports that "‥, according to ECB estimates, our monetary policy measures have contributed to reducing euro-area long-term risk-free rates by around 80 basis points since June 2014. Asset purchases have contributed significantly to this drop and have therefore been an indispensable tool to create the financial conditions necessary for inflation to move back towards levels consistent with price stability",[14] said Benoit Coeuré in a speech in Frankfurt on May 16, 2017.

[13] Allianz (2016b).

[14] Coeuré (2017, p. 2); see also ECB (2017) and Praet (2017).

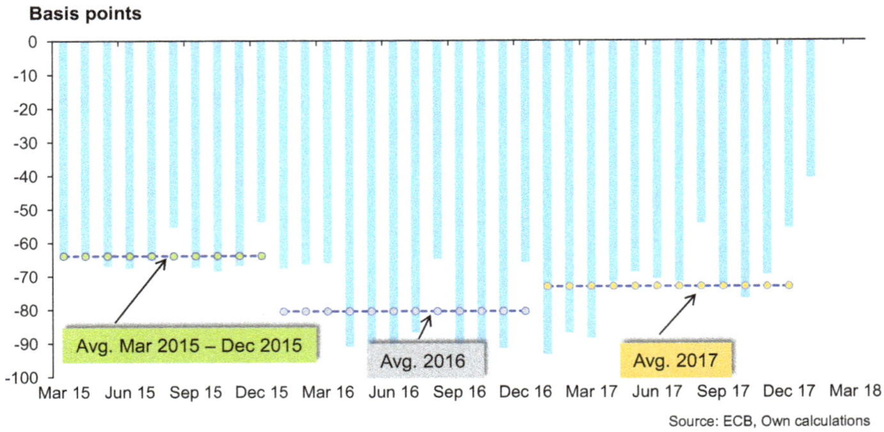


**Fig. 2.13** Estimated QE impact on 10-year German government bond yields (Mar 2015 to Jan 2018)

This discussion about the influence that central banks have on interest rate expectations and the term premium begs the question whether they have more or less full control over longer-term bond yields. The policies of the Bank of Japan, which introduced a strategy of yield curve control, are often taken as evidence that this is, in principle, possible. But there are some caveats. The capacity of a central bank to influence bond yields depends on the credibility of its forward guidance and on the risk assessments of bond investors. If market participants come to the view that inflation is emerging, very loose monetary policy and low interest rate promises will not be credible. Moreover, in times of reemerging inflation, interest rate volatility will rise and long-term bonds will become riskier. In such an environment, long-term bondholders will not accept zero or even negative term premia. Japan's monetary policy has been credible since inflation was clearly below target for a very long period of time and deflationary risks were evident. Also, the huge amounts of additional bonds issued by the government are mainly held domestically by private households, the central bank and Japanese financial institutions. If these conditions were to change significantly through higher inflation or downward pressure on the currency, Yen-investments would become much less attractive, and yield curve control at least at a level close to zero would become virtually impossible.

The question how effectively central banks can influence bond yields is also relevant for a situation in which they seek to achieve an upward correction. There have been a few occasions when it was difficult for monetary policy to increase long-term yield in order to reduce monetary stimulus. The most widely known "interest rate conundrum" is the one stated by former Fed Chairman Alan Greenspan. He noted that while the Fed had increased the Fed funds rate from 1% in June 2004 to 5.25% in 18 consecutive steps until July 2006, the yields of 10-year bonds hardly increased during this period of time. Foreign purchases of US bonds are seen as one of the main reasons for this development.[15] Similarly, in 2017 and 2018 the Fed's interest rate hikes did not strongly move long term yields upward but mainly led to a flattening of the yield curve. Despite the reduction in monetary accommodation, many indicators like stock prices, corporate yield spreads or volatility showed loosening rather than tightening monetary conditions. Interest rate expectations (and inflation expectations) of market participants were consistently below central bank governors' projections in 2017, keeping the longer-term bond yields rather low. A major explanation for this "paradox of tightening"[16] is to be found in the global financial context and the linkages between the markets for safe assets in the US, the euro area and Japan. As the ECB and the BoJ were pursuing extremely accommodative policies and engaging in large-scale asset purchases in 2017, there was significant investor demand for higher yielding Treasuries and therefore, the Fed tightening had only a very limited impact on long-term Treasuries.[17]

In conclusion, central banks have a significant impact on, but certainly no full control over bond yields. In recent years, central banks' forward guidance indicating low rates has usually coincided with rather gloomy market expectations concerning growth and inflation. These expectations are likely to change in coming years. Should markets return to higher inflation expectations as inflation continues to normalize, this will push up bond yields as well. In case of higher inflation, the term premia in bond yields will also rise from their, still, exceptionally low levels, especially in the euro area. Higher risk premia will be supported by the phasing out of the ECB's large-scale asset purchase program and further balance sheet reduction by the Fed. Central banks should tolerate a rise of term premia, as the deflationary threat has been overcome. An adequate risk premium is important for efficient capital allocation. Long-term bonds definitely do have higher valuation risks and higher volatility than short-term bonds. Investors and savers should be compensated for these risks with a positive premium.

[15] Craine and Martin (2009).

[16] BIS (2017b).

[17] Heise (2017).

## References

Allianz (2016a) Brandmeir K, Grimm M, Heise M, Holzhausen A. Global wealth report 2016

Allianz (2016b) Hanenberg C, Schneider R. An interest rate model for the Eurozone and the US (Working Paper No. 204)

Allianz (2017) Brandmeir K, Grimm M, Heise M, Holzhausen A. Global wealth report 2017

Bain and Company (2018) Harris K, Kimson A, Schwedel A. Labour 2030: the collision of demographics, automation and inequality

Bernanke BS (2013) Long-term interest rates. Speech presented at the Annual Monetary/Macroeconomics Conference in San Francisco, CA

BIS (2017a) Bank of international settlements. 87th annual report

BIS (2017b) Bank for international settlements. BIS Quarterly Review December 2017: a paradoxical tightening?

Borio C, Disyatat P, Juselius M, Rungcharoenkitkul P (2017) Why so low for so long? A long-term view of real interest rates (Working Paper No. 685). Monetary and Economic Department, BIS

Coeuré B (2017) Dissecting the yield curve: a central bank perspective. Speech presented at the annual meeting of the ECB's Bond Market Contact Group in Frankfurt am Main, Germany on May 16

Craine R, Martin VL (2009) Interest rate conundrum. BE J Macroecon 9(1):1–27

Deutsche Bundesbank (2017) The natural rate of interest. Monthly Report October 2017, 69(10)

Draghi M (2015) The ECB's recent monetary policy measures, effectiveness and challenges. Lecture presented at the Camdessus Lecture of the IMF in Washington, DC on May 14

Draghi M (2017) Monetary policy and the outlook for the economy. Speech presented at the Frankfurt European Banking Congress in Frankfurt am Main, Germany on November 17

European Central Bank (2017) Annual Report 2016

Ferrero G, Gross M, Neri S (2017) On secular stagnation and low interest rates: demography matters (Working Paper No. 2088). European Central Bank

German Council of Economic Advisors (2015) Executive office of the President of the United States, long-term interest rates: a survey

German Council of Economic Experts (2016) Annual report 2016/2017: time for reforms

German Council of Economic Experts (2017) Annual report 2017/2018: towards a forward-looking economic policy, Ch.4 & Ch.5

Heise M (2017) Fed's failure to tighten financial conditions a cause for concern. Financial Times, December 13

Heise M, Langenegger, J, Schneider R (2016) Low real interest rates: causes and outlook (Working paper No. 197). Allianz

Holston K, Laubach T, Wilson J C (2016) Measuring the natural rate of interest: international trends and determinants (Working Paper No. 2016-11) Federal Reserve Bank of San Francisco

Laubach T, Williams JC (2001) Measuring the natural rate of interest. Board of Governors of the Federal Reserve System

Lemke W, Werner T (2017) Dissecting long-term Bund yields in the run-up to the ECB's Public Sector Purchase Programme (Working Paper No. 2106) European Central Bank

Michaelis H, Wieland V (2017) R-Star and the Draghi rules: correctly measuring the equilibrium interest rate for policy use. VoxEU

Powell JH (2018) Monetary policy in a changing economy. Speech presented at the "Changing market structure and implications for monetary policy" symposium of the Federal Reserve Bank of Kansas City. Jackson Hole, WY, August 24

Praet P (2017) Maintaining price stability with nonconventional monetary policy measures. Speech presented at the SUERF Conference, New York City, NY, October 11

Rachel L, Smith TD (2015) Secular drivers of the global real interest rate (Staff Working Paper No. 571). Bank of England

Taylor JB, Wieland V (2016) Finding the equilibrium real interest rate in a fog of policy deviations. Institute for Monetary and Financial Stability (Working Paper Series No. 103), Goethe University Frankfurt am Main

# 3

# Uncertainties About the Monetary Transmission Mechanism

*The transmission mechanism of QE is itself not fully understood and remains controversial, so that the impact of tapering, ending and reversing the process is as yet unknown. Here it is important to understand that we are not simply dealing with risk, but with uncertainty. Risk denotes the infamous "known unknowns". Uncertainty, on the other hand, denotes the unknown unknowns. Uncertainty means ignorance about the underlying mechanism, about the probability distribution and—even worse—about the potential outcomes. So how to explain the discrepancy between very high uncertainty and financial market complacency? Markets are very good at discovering, trading, pricing and insuring risks, but they are not good at mapping the unpredictable nature of politics. Uncertainty—by definition—cannot be priced. That's why markets often ignore it and take a wait-and-see approach. Today's low financial market volatilities are deceptive and underestimate the underlying risks—or rather, uncertainties. Investors and policymakers should enjoy the upswing while it lasts, since it will not last.*

Axel Weber, Financial Times, January 8, 2018

**Abstract** Having analyzed the impact of monetary policy on bond-yields, this chapter now looks at its impact on growth and inflation. For the design of any monetary policy strategy, understanding the channels by which monetary stimulus is transmitted into the real economy is key. Without reliable and foreseeable patterns of influence on aggregate demand and inflation, monetary policies would be like sailing without navigation. In recent years central banks have grappled with significant uncertainty surrounding the strength of various transmission channels. The impact on credit demand and supply via the so-called credit or banking channels was very weak in the years after the financial crisis. Companies and households made it a priority to


M. Heise, *Inflation Targeting and Financial Stability*,
https://doi.org/10.1007/978-3-030-05078-8_3

repair their balance sheets. Central banks did manage to push up asset prices, and induce investors to rebalance their portfolios towards riskier assets (via the portfolio channel). Exchange rate changes have taken place, but not always in the expected direction. Whether, and if so to what extent, these effects have been conducive to overall growth is debatable, especially as significant side effects on financial stability and retirement assets need to be taken into account. Furthermore, the fact that even ultra-expansionary monetary policies could not lift inflation towards the targets suggest that domestic factors are becoming relatively less important for inflation than international ones, such as swings in commodity prices, global excess production capacity or hyper-competition in global goods and labor markets. Despite reams of research, our understanding of the transmission effects of monetary policy remains imperfect.

## 3.1 The Credit Channel in Times of Deleveraging[1]

An important path of monetary transmission runs through the commercial banking system.[2] Central banks can alter short-term borrowing or deposit conditions and the amount of liquidity or base money available to the banking system. It depends on actions by the banks, however, to what extent such a stimulus will be passed on to clients and thereby generate additional demand in the economy. The decision of a commercial bank to lower borrowing rates for their clients and raise the amount of lending depends on many issues besides central bank policies. Most importantly, banks can lend to the private sector only if they are adequately capitalized and meet regulatory requirements (solvency requirements, liquidity ratios, total loss rules). So the pass-through of monetary policy action is in no way guaranteed; it will depend quite heavily on risk-taking capabilities of the banking system.

Further uncertainties emerge as the interest rate approaches the zero lower bound. In such a situation central banks resort to unconventional measures of monetary policy, such as large-scale asset purchases or negative interest rates. The idea behind such measures is to reduce the duration risk in banks' balance

[1] Next to the literature cited in the text, research on the various transmission channels can be found in Thornton (2014), Buttz et al. (2015), Joyce et al. (2015), Hesse et al. (2017), and Quint and Rabanal (2017).

[2] For an overview of monetary transmissions channels see Mishkin (2018).

sheets and to incentivize them to use the liquidity gained by asset sales—be it from their own portfolios or in commission for clients—for extending more loans or buying higher yielding corporate assets. Whether this will happen depends on various factors that will shape banks' expectations, e.g. the expected persistence of the liquidity, the adequacy of lending spreads and the availability of risk capital. It also depends on the demand side of the credit market. If borrowers are constrained by a lack of capital or collateral, the stimulus of the central bank may simply peter out. Looking at the build-up of huge (and costly) cash balances of the banks in the Eurosystem in the years after the great financial crisis and the lack of significant credit growth for many years, there is compelling evidence that the credit channel was not working properly.

The first factor that hampered the credit channel of monetary stimulus after the crisis was capital shortages in the banking system. Inadequate capital reserves forced banks to decrease risks and repair their balance sheets. A process of de-leveraging and de-risking set in. Banks scrutinized and reduced their loan books, offloaded investments that bound capital and tightened credit standards for new loans. After a crisis like the one in 2008, such balance sheet repair is a matter of survival and it will take place even if there is a lot of cheap central bank liquidity available.

Conversely, on the side of borrowers, be they corporate or household clients, the fallout from a financial crisis tends to trigger risk reduction and spending restraint. After the great financial crisis, the average credit quality of bank clients declined. Financial assets were impaired and many private borrowers threatened by job losses or at least lower incomes. In such a situation, monetary policy will not be very effective via the credit channel. All it can do is to smooth the process of de-leveraging and extend it over a longer period of time. This can help limit immediate adjustment pressures after a financial shock, but it also carries major economic risks if it slows down balance sheet adjustments for too long. If loans are continuously extended to weak borrowers, such policies will not accelerate growth but slow it down, since weak and highly leveraged companies do not usually invest, innovate and generate growth. Central banks must therefore also have an eye on the "forbearance" in loan policies to prevent keeping "zombie companies" alive.[3]

[3] Storz et al. (2017).

**Zombie firms.** "Zombie firms" can be broadly defined as companies that are unprofitable over an extended period of time and cannot cover debt servicing costs from current profits. Recent research [see e.g., Adalet McGowan et al. (2017) and Banerjee and Hofmann (2018)] indicates that the prevalence of such companies as a share of the total population of non-financial companies has increased significantly in the wake of the Great Financial Crisis across advanced economies.

Banerjee and Hofmann from the BIS explore the rise of "zombie companies" in an international perspective covering 14 advanced economies by using the Worldscope database of 32,000 companies. They focus on listed companies and consider two different ways of identifying zombie firms: a *broad* measure proposed by Adalet McGowan based on persistent lack of profitability in mature firms; and a *narrow* one which additionally requires expectations of low future profitability inferred from a firm's stock market valuation.

The authors summarize their key findings as follows:

- The prevalence of zombie firms has ratcheted up since the late 1980s.
- This appears to be linked to reduced financial pressure, reflecting in part the effects of lower interest rates.
- Zombie firms are less productive and crowd out investment in and employment at more productive firms.
- When identifying zombie firms, it appears to be important to take into account expected future profitability in addition to weak past performance.

A number of factors can make zombie firms survive for a long time. For one, the design of the insolvency regime in the respective country is important. If poorly designed, insolvency rules can inhibit the process of corporate restructuring. Another important factor is the strength and capital adequacy of banks. When banks' balance sheets are weakened by a financial crisis and they cannot "afford" the write-off of impaired loans, they have an incentive to roll over loans to non-viable firms and buy time. This type of behavior also inhibits the process of corporate restructuring in the economy.

The prevalence of zombie firms can also be attributed to the downward trend in interest rates. Lower interest rate expenses reduce the pressure on the firms and possibly also their lenders to clean up balance sheets and instead make them "evergreen" their loans to weak companies. Furthermore, in an environment of low interest rates, investors will have a higher risk appetite. This can reduce financial pressures on weak companies.

The data analyzed by Banerjee and Hofmann suggests that the share of zombie firms is negatively correlated with both bank health and interest rates. However, they find that lower nominal interest rates have a stronger predictive impact on the number of zombie firms than indicators of bank health.

Their findings confirm other studies that have shown zombie companies to weaken economic performance (Caballero et al. 2008; Adalet McGowan et al. 2017). On average, labour productivity and total factor productivity of such firms are lower than those of their peers, thereby leading to a weaker macroeconomic development. With a significant share of "zombie firms", capital is not allocated effectively and less resources are available for non-zombie companies, reducing their investment activity.

What do these considerations imply for policy makers in central banks? They certainly have difficult decisions to take. In the midst of a financial crisis, the highest priority of central banks is to restore confidence amongst financial actors and stabilize the whole system. Some forbearance in lending policies might be acceptable. But to kick-start a recovery of economic activity it is necessary that banks write down bad loans and recapitalize. They need to be able to supply funds to firms that generate higher productivity and investment. Smoothing the process of balance sheet adjustment for too long will therefore be counter-productive for long-term growth.

Some evidence of such a counter-productive process can be seen in Japan after the bubble burst in 1989. A policy of extreme monetary accommodation was designed to support the banking system. In the end, it led to a long delay in the balance sheet adjustments of financial institutions that were inevitable in the long-run. The process finally did take place in the wake of the Japanese financial sector reform in 1997. Richard Koo,[4] the Nomura economist who coined the term of a balance sheet recession, argues that monetary policy is the first casualty of such a development. The attempt to stimulate new lending cannot be successful when there are not enough borrowers. The risk is that a policy focused primarily on lending will just keep weak firms alive. In line with this reasoning, the unprecedented surge of central bank liquidity which the Bank of Japan has generated over the years has not led to major growth of credit or money holdings in the private sector (Fig. 3.1).

Reproducing Koo's Japan chart for the US (Fig. 3.2) and the euro area (Fig. 3.3) shows a similar picture. Despite the massive balance sheet expansion of the respective central banks, the amount of bank lending grew only moderately or even declined, as in the Eurozone after the financial crisis of 2008. The liquidity the monetary authorities provided to banks at extremely low interest rates did not generate strong investment and credit demand in the private sector. In the US, the total volume of credit in the non-financial private sector fell in relation to nominal GDP from 2009 until 2012. Since then it has been rising again. In Europe the decline of credit ratios lasted until 2016. European banks' balance sheets declined considerably during this period. Two factors probably explain why financial flows adjusted more quickly in the US: First, US authorities enforced a recapitalization of banks and the off-loading of bad loans faster and more forcefully than their European counterparts. The stability of banks is crucial for the impact of monetary policy through the credit channel. Second, in the USA's much more market

[4] Koo (2011), see also Koo (2016) and Takahashi (2013).

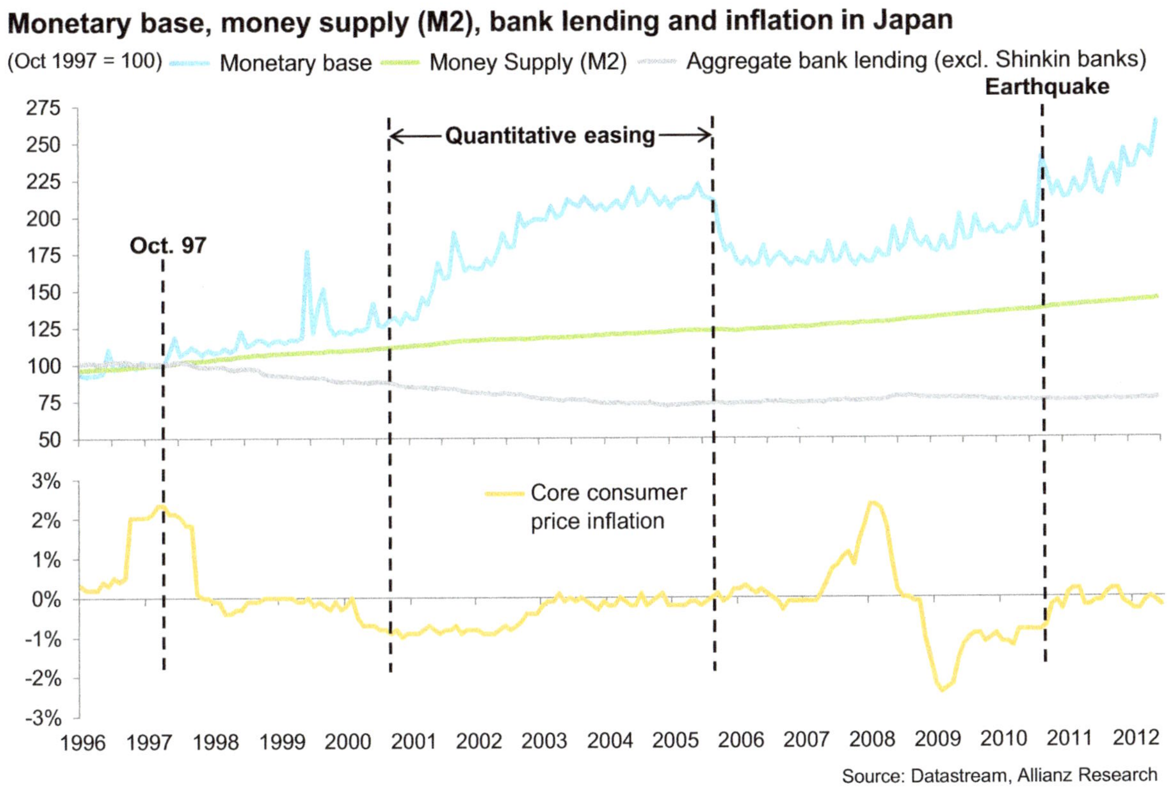


**Fig. 3.1** Drastic liquidity injection without much effect in Japan

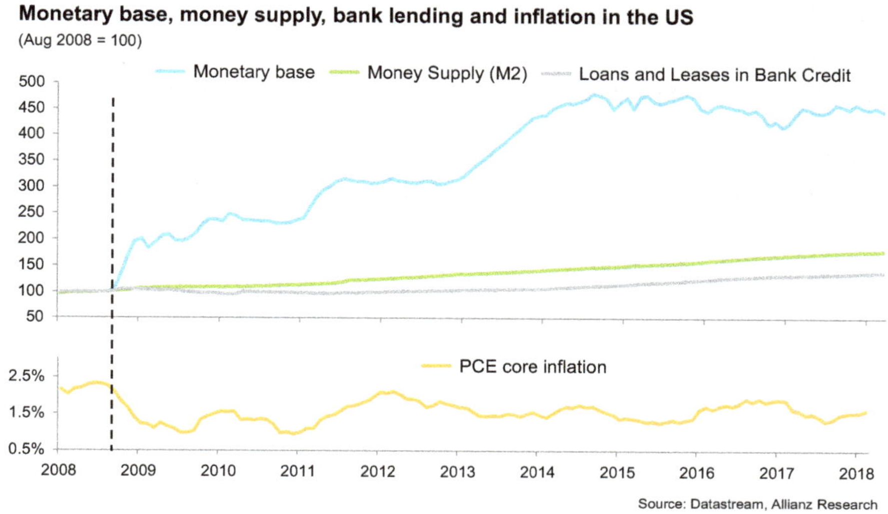


**Fig. 3.2** Moderate increase of bank lending despite quantitative easing in the US

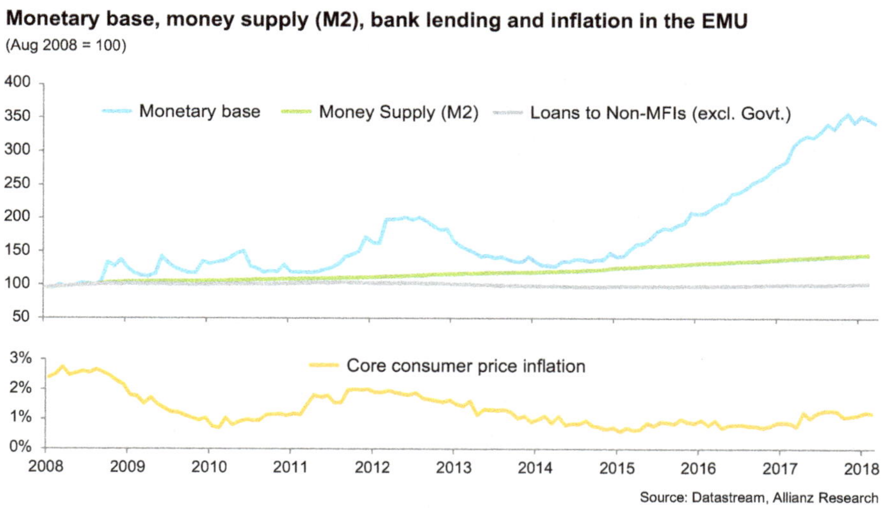


**Fig. 3.3** Weak Eurozone bank lending despite balance sheet expansion by the ECB

based financial system, an asset purchase program that included large amounts of mortgage backed securities as well as government and corporate bonds had a stronger effect on financial conditions than in Europe's more bank-based system. In Europe, banks' balance sheets have a much bigger role in financing the economy. Therefore, when banks suffer capital shortages, monetary policy transmission is significantly weakened. These factors help to explain why the credit cycle turned at an earlier point in the US than in the eurozone. What is more, the euro area debt crisis led to a slump in the currency union's growth, compounding the above mentioned factors.

In the meantime, even in the euro area conditions for bank lending have improved considerably. With banks being better capitalized and private borrowers again taking more risks, the instruments of monetary policy for incentivizing lending have again become more effective. However, in an economic and financial upswing, there is no need for the central bank to incentivize more leverage in the economy. Rather, the central bank should focus on dampening the buildup of risks that could eventually backfire when the economy slows and financial markets go into reverse after a boom (see Sect. 4.3).

## 3.2 The Risks Involved in the Asset Price Channel

Central banks, with their interest rate and liquidity policies, may not have been able to prevent the downturn in the credit cycle in the years after the financial crisis. But, with a combination of conventional and unconventional policies they have helped to relieve financial constraints in the private sector. They brought about rising valuations of bonds, equities and real estate, which in turn improved banks' capital ratios as well as the value of collateral that borrowers could offer. Thus they alleviated the de-risking pressures that the economies faced after the financial crisis.

In general terms, the impact of central bank policies on asset prices depends on the portfolio adjustments after such interventions. They can take place in banks' balance sheets, which use abundant and low interest yielding liquidity to purchase more risk-bearing assets. They can also occur in the non-bank sector, where institutional investors like pension funds, insurance companies, foundations or private and public wealth funds re-allocate their portfolios from low interest bearing bonds and cash to higher yielding assets. Such re-allocations push up the prices of stocks, corporate bonds and real assets like real estate. The impact of monetary policy will be stronger the longer investors expect (safe) bond yields to stay low. Cash-flows from longer dated assets will then be discounted at a lower rate.

Quantifying the impact of monetary policy on asset valuations is difficult. There are numerous other factors that play a role for asset prices—basically anything that changes the economic outlook and return expectations. As we cannot construct clear counter-factual scenarios that would show financial market developments without monetary policy stimulus, we cannot determine the effect with any empirical accuracy. It is plausible, however, that accommodative monetary policies of the past years have had a rather strong impact on financial market valuations and real estate prices. Markets have proved to be resilient to significant political shocks. Neither the Brexit vote and the election of President Trump nor continued uncertainties in Italy, to name just a few examples, derailed the upswing in financial markets. Market participants were confident that monetary policy would respond to possible market disruptions, thereby creating the "buy-the-dip" mentality. In this sense monetary policy suppressed market volatility during the years after the financial crisis. Since the Fed has begun to withdraw its stimulus, and the ECB has at least announced a normalization of policy, such sentiments appear to have changed.

Higher asset prices have been the main driver of financial household wealth in recent years. Over the past 5 years, for example, asset price gains have contributed more strongly to the growth of global financial wealth than new private savings (Fig. 3.4). In the US, over 70% of the growth of financial

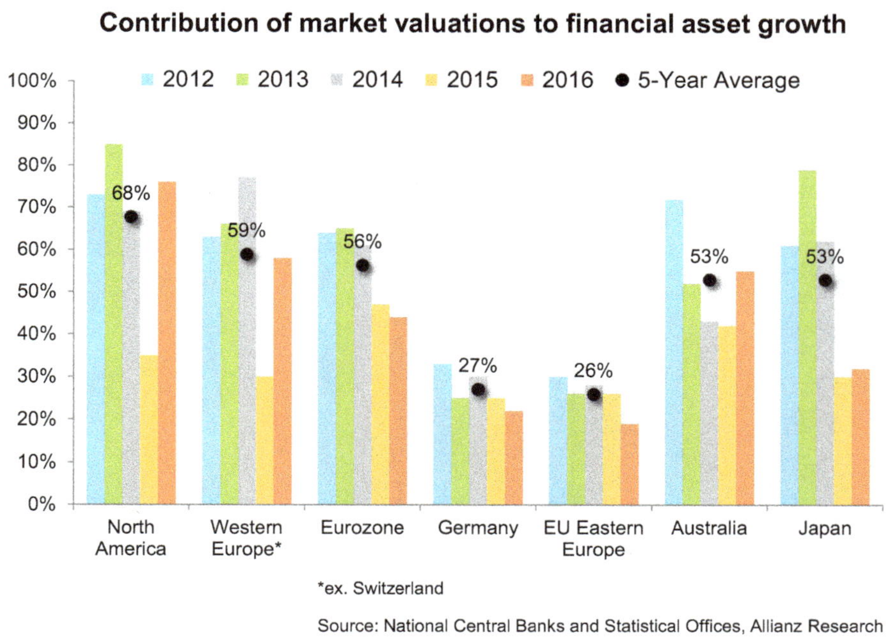


**Fig. 3.4** How valuation gains impact financial wealth

assets (bank deposits, securities pensions and life insurance) was generated by valuation gains. In the euro area, where households hold less of their money in securities and more in bank accounts, the impact of rising asset prices was somewhat lower, but still substantial, at 50%. In Germany this figure is significantly lower. Here, the large share of bank deposits, insurance and pension products as well as relatively moderate valuation gains on German bond holdings kept the impact on asset price movements at about 20% of gross financial wealth in the past 5 years.

These figures on gross financial wealth do not include real estate, which accounts for a huge chunk of overall household wealth. In the OECD's countries, wealth from real estate even exceeds that from financial assets. Real estate prices tend to be sensitive to interest rate changes and hence react significantly to changes in monetary policy. Not surprisingly, real estate prices have boomed in recent years, and in both the US and EU prices far exceeded their 2007 levels in 2018 (Figs. 3.5 and 3.6).

Such gains in financial assets and real estate will, on balance, have a positive effect on demand. As households feel richer, they tend to consume more. In the corporate sector, companies will benefit from higher equity and better collateral, which has a positive effect on financing conditions. Banks are better capitalized when markets are up and volatility is low. Financial constraints on lending activities are loosened.

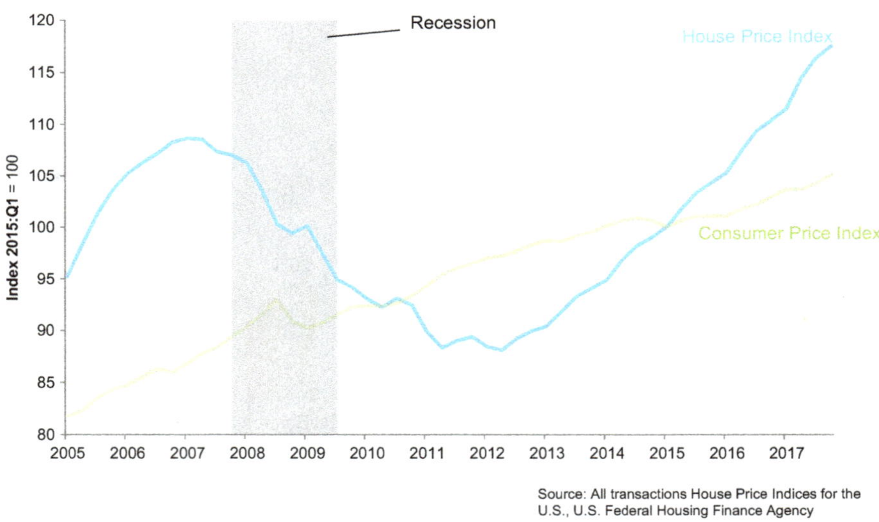


**Fig. 3.5** House price index USA

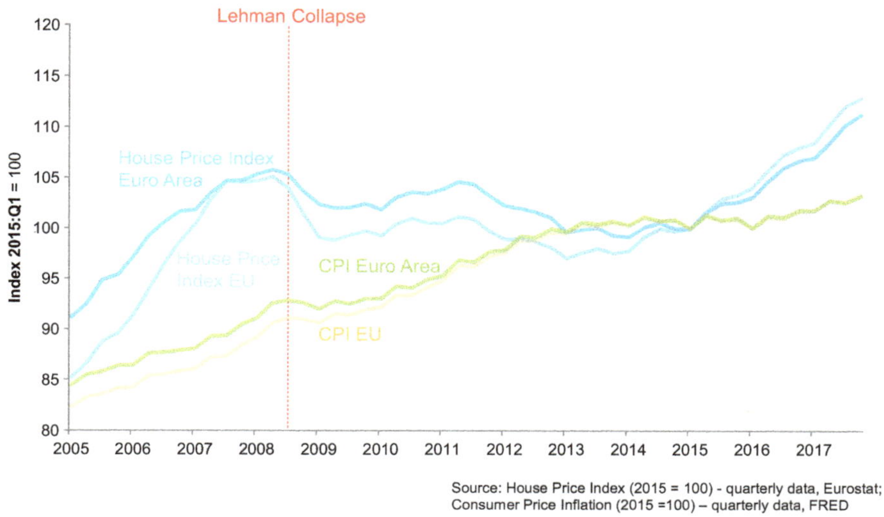


**Fig. 3.6** House price index Europe

But these positive first-round effects of policy-induced asset price gains can be counteracted by secondary effects of monetary stimulus policies (or side-effects, to be analyzed in Chap. 4). For instance, the increase of bond prices and stock valuations will reduce investors' expectation of future rates of return. Projections concerning the growth of long-term savings, such as pension assets or life insurance claims, will be lowered. With lower future returns, savers have to increase their savings efforts to reach aspired income streams. Household consumption and investment may go down. In economic jargon, the negative income effect of lower capital returns can outweigh the so-called substitution effect, which implies that households increasingly prefer consumption over saving when interest rates are low.

Saving rates in the corporate sector can also increase, as companies need to replenish capital reserves in their occupational pension schemes to avoid reducing promised payouts for their retirees. Such moves divert funds away from real investment for business expansion. These effects help to explain why savings activity, as Fig. 2.3 shows, stayed much higher than the drastic fall in interest rates after the financial crisis might have suggested. That is true also for the more recent years, when the ECB started its large-scale asset purchases and tried to stimulate consumption via negative interest rates. As savings rates remained high, this has certainly limited the impact of monetary accommodation on growth.

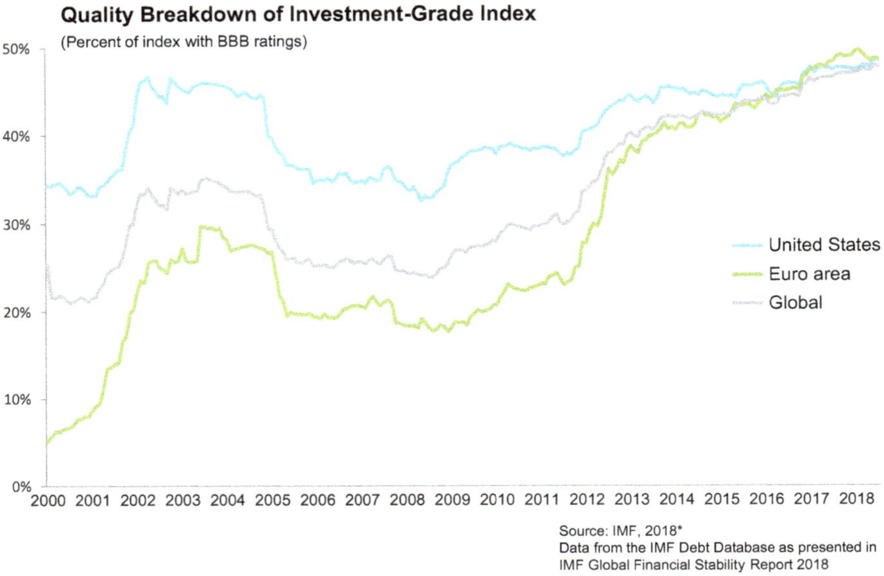


**Fig. 3.7** Balance sheet vulnerabilities

What is more, investors, in particular those who are not heavily regulated, have achieved relatively high returns in recent years by taking higher risks. The boom of leveraged loans, the growth of structured products like Collateralized Loan Obligations (CLOs) and the remarkable growth of Electronic Traded Funds (ETFs), to name only a few examples, are evidence of this higher risk exposure. Furthermore, the issuance of triple B bonds is growing quickly and the share of such bonds in the universe of investment grade bonds is increasing, as the IMF shows in its recent Global Financial Stability Report (Fig. 3.7).[5]

For the euro area, corporate bond portfolios of asset managers also show a declining share of high quality bonds and more risks in their portfolios (Fig. 3.8). If and when the macroeconomic outlook worsens and investors become more risk averse again, the value of lower quality bonds will decline disproportionately. The positive effects that asset prices had on consumer and investment demand will then turn strongly negative and amplify the economic slowdown. The same can happen when the interest rate outlook changes and central banks become more hawkish. Then, the return on safe bonds will rise while markets for lower quality assets suffer.

[5] IMF (2018a).

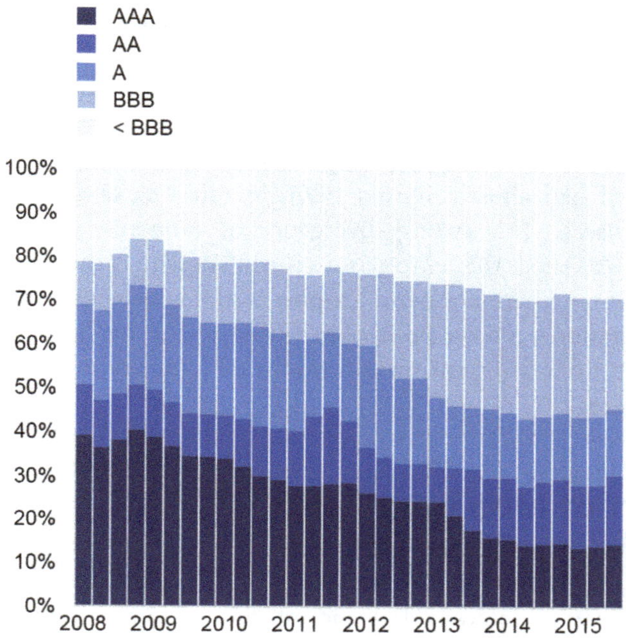


Source: ESRB, Macroprudential policy issues arising from low interest rates and structural changes in the EU financial system, Nov. 2016

**Fig. 3.8** Corporate bond holdings under asset management in the eurozone by rating

In its recent Global Financial Stability Report, the IMF shows that expansionary monetary policies can also make investors adjust the shares of foreign and domestic assets in their portfolios. When domestic asset prices are increasing across various markets, investors will look abroad for more attractive returns. The resulting capital outflows can push down the exchange rate of the country in question.[6] The exchange rate impact of monetary accommodation can stimulate the economy through higher net exports, and thereby reinforce the domestic policy impact. However, exchange rate changes are not a reliable transmission mechanism for monetary policy. First, deliberate devaluation strategies run counter to the interest of trading partners. The latter may accuse their partner of currency manipulation and adopt retaliatory measures. A downward spiral of competitive devaluations benefits nobody whilst it introducing an expansionary bias in global monetary policies. Therefore, the ECB

[6] A more detailed discussion of the relevant effects can be found in Coeuré (2017).

and other western central banks have repeatedly ruled out policies that target the exchange rate for the purposes of competitiveness. Secondly, the impact of monetary policies on the exchange is anything but clear-cut. Why, for example, did the dollar fall against the euro from December 2016 to April 2018, despite the fact that Eurozone monetary policy remained extremely expansionary whereas the Fed had already started hiking interest rates and had stopped its asset purchases? This strong divergence of monetary policies should have further weakened the euro vis-a-vis the dollar, rather than strengthening it. Of course, there are many ex-post explanations for this—changing growth expectations, reserve policies in China and so on—but the example still shows that monetary transmission via the exchange rate channel is not really a viable strategy.

## 3.3 The Impact of Monetary Policy and the Phillips Curve Debate

> The link between measures of domestic slack and inflation has proved rather weak and elusive for at least a couple of decades now. True, if one tries hard enough, it is always possible to find it. But it is not the kind of relationship that jumps out at you and appears robust. Indeed, this is a recurrent theme in the discussions at the central bankers' meetings in Basel. Claudio Borio, head of the BIS Monetary and Economic Department, 2017, p. 2.

The bottom line from previous chapters is that a lot of uncertainty surrounds the workings of the monetary transmission mechanism, not only with regard to traditional interest rate and refinancing policies, but even more so for large-scale asset purchase programs. The failure of even radical steps of monetary policy to ignite higher inflation can be seen in Fig. 3.9. There is no clear pattern between the ECB's unconventional measures and the development of inflation. Actually, inflation fell quite drastically in the years from 2011 to 2015, despite forceful ECB intervention.

This lack of clear impact raises the question whether narrow and precisely defined inflation targets are appropriate. One might argue, as central banks do, that inflation and GDP growth would have been even weaker in the years after the crisis without monetary accommodation. The ECB, for example, calculates that its accommodative policies pushed up inflation by a full 0.5

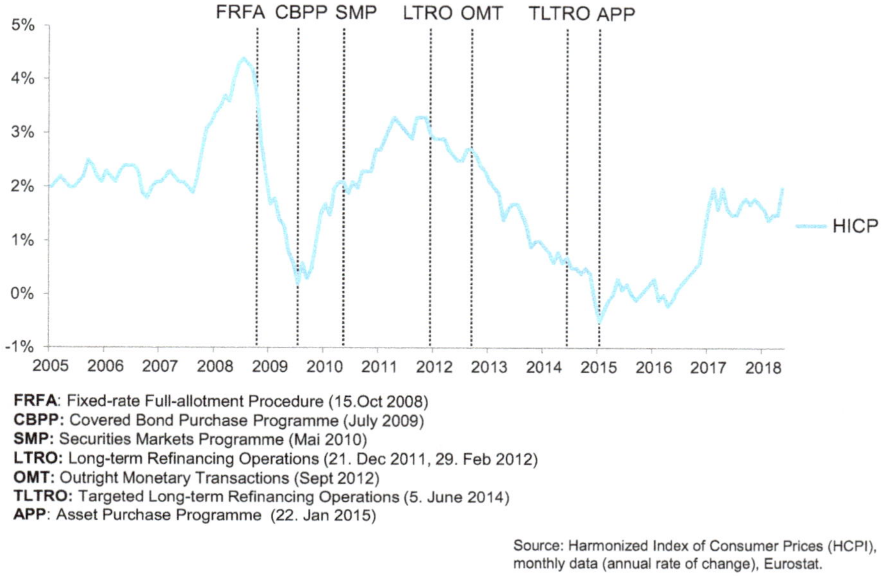


**Fig. 3.9** ECB policy measures and the harmonized index of consumer prices

percentage points in 2016.[7] To underpin such arguments, central bankers and economists use models to generate scenarios of the economy under different assumption about the stance of monetary policies. Different models and methods, however, produce diverging results. Some studies look at signaling effects of monetary policy by analyzing changes in financial variables, such as bond yields, equities or exchange rates, immediately after monetary policy announcements. Other studies use time series (VAR) techniques to see how monetary policy shapes output and inflation, next to other factors.[8] Finally, macroeconomic equilibrium models and interest rate term structure models have produced a wide variety of results, depending on model specification, assumptions and estimation techniques. The widely used new Keynesian macroeconomic equilibrium models, which incorporate rational expectations, still involve assumptions that can be questioned. First, they assume that the so-called interest rate gap—that is the difference between market rates, which central banks can influence, and equilibrium rates, which generate full employment and stable inflation—affects the rate of capacity utilization, the

[7] Praet (2016) and ECB (2016). A wide range of estimates for the effect of monetary accommodation on inflation in the eurozone can be found in Deutsche Bundesbank (2016a, b).

[8] Researchers have employed VAR and structural models, see also Gambetti and Musso (2017).

so-called output gap in the economy. Secondly, in this line of thinking, the output gap determines the rate of inflation.

The latter relationship is the traditional Phillips curve, which seems to have been upended in recent years. In the great recession after the financial crisis, inflation at first remained rather high. During the subsequent recovery and expansion, inflation turned out to be lower than the considerable increase in resource utilization in the US and strongly falling unemployment would have suggested. In other words, the Phillips curve relationship seems to have become rather weak.

Accordingly, several economists and central bankers, including the former chairwoman of the US-Fed, Janet Yellen,[9] have started questioning our understanding of inflation dynamics. Various possible explanations for the 'end of the Phillips curve' have been be put forward. One is that the measurement of the output gap is distorted or that official unemployment measures do not capture the true level of unemployment, because many people are working part-time or have retreated from the labor market due to a lack of employment opportunities. Another is that inflation expectations may have become well anchored and less responsive to the slack in the economy as central banks' anti-inflation policies have gained credibility. With well-anchored, stable inflation expectations, wage demands are more likely to remain moderate even in a situation of low unemployment.

These explanations have some merit. In addition, however, global trends increasingly influence domestic price developments. Globalization and increasing openness have rendered domestic developments in demand and capacity utilization less important for inflation. Instead, import prices affect domestic inflation more strongly, as the share of imports has risen in all advanced economies. Also, increasing competition from China and other emerging economies in labor-intensive industries has limited the room that companies have for setting prices and responding to wage requests. The integration of China and the former Soviet countries into the global economy has added around 1.6 billion people to the global labor force in the last three decades.

In parallel, radical advances in digital technology have allowed companies to globalize and have made markets much more transparent. These technologies have facilitated global value chains and the relocation of production of goods and services across the world, also enabling a surge of international capital flows. Therefore, we should not overestimate central banks' ability to

[9] See for example Yellen (2017).

fine-tune inflation. The Phillips curve relationship between (national) capacity utilization and inflation has, thus, not completely disappeared, but it has become weaker.

**Inflation in emerging markets**. At this point it is important to note that there are differences in the drivers of inflation between advanced and emerging economies. In its recent World Economic Outlook, the IMF points to the importance of inflation expectations for actual inflation performance in emerging economies. Deviations of inflation from target are mainly caused by fluctuations in longer-term inflation expectations. The role of global factors in determining inflation is seen to be more limited (although commodity prices do play a large role for most emerging markets). In recent years there has been progress in anchoring inflation expectations, not least due to policies of inflation targeting, and that has helped to reduce inflation to low and sustainable levels. Whether these gains will be maintained, the Fund writes, "largely depends on policymakers' continued commitment to improving the long-term sustainability of fiscal frameworks, including by adopting fiscal rules, and preserving and rebuilding fiscal buffers where necessary. Equally important is their commitment to improving the credibility of central banks, which can be achieved by consolidating and enhancing their independence, as well as through improvements in timeliness, clarity, transparency, and openness in communications" (IMF 2018b, p. 117). The anchoring of inflation expectations is extremely important at a time when monetary policy normalizes in advanced economies. Emerging markets with less well-anchored inflation expectations have recently come under considerable pressures from exchange rate depreciations and shorter-term inflation. Here, continued improvements in fiscal and monetary policy frameworks are needed, hence inflation targeting can be a helpful tool.

Another important relationship that features strongly in the widely used (new) Keynesian macroeconomic models is the assumption that changes in policy rates affect aggregate demand and the output gap in a significant and predictable way. In recent years, this has not been evident. Falling policy rates and declining bond yields did not seem to trigger faster growth of investment demand and consumption in advanced economies.[10] In particular, as shown in Sect. 3.1, neither investment ratios nor savings ratios reacted to the marked fall of interest rates in larger developed economies, as banks and non-financial firms were operating under strong balance sheet constraints that rendered the level of interest rates less important. The impact of low interest rates on households' financial position has been ambiguous (see Chap. 4). While rising asset prices added to the wealth of those who invested in securities or real assets,

[10] This development seemed to be a reminder of a situation where the Keynesian liquidity trap and an interest inelastic investment schedule coincide.

those who held their money in bank accounts and other forms of liquidity saw their interest income evaporate. Also, the return on safe investments, such as long-term pension products decreased. Therefore, it is not surprising that savings ratios did not decline in line with lower interest rates. Lower rates of return may have made savers worry that their long-term savings accounts and retirement assets would be insufficient to generate enough income in the future. This called for continuously high or even higher savings efforts especially by the generations close to retirement.

## References

Adalet McGowan M, Andrews D, Millot V (2017) The walking dead: zombie firms and productivity performance in OECD countries (OECD Economics Department Working Papers No 1372)

Banerjee R, Hofmann B (2018) The rise of zombie firms: causes and consequences. BIS Quarterly Review

Borio C (2017) Through the looking glass. OMFIF City Lecture, September 22

Buttz N, Churmz R, McMahon M, Morotzz A, Schanz J (2015) QE and the bank lending channel in the United Kingdom (Bank of England Working Paper No. 511)

Caballero R, Hoshi T, Kashyap A (2008) Zombie lending and depressed restructuring in Japan. Am Econ Rev 98(5):1943–1977

Coeuré B (2017) Monetary policy, exchange rates and capital flows. Speech presented at the 18th Jacques Polak Annual Research Conference hosted by the IMF in Washington, DC on November 3

Deutsche Bundesbank (2016a) The Phillips curve as an instrument for analyzing prices and forecasting inflation in Germany. Monthly Report April 2016, 68(4)

Deutsche Bundesbank (2016b) The macroeconomic impact of quantitative easing in the euro area. Monthly Report June 2016, 68(6)

European Central Bank (2016) Annual report 2015

Gambetti L, Musso A (2017) The macroeconomic impact of the ECB's expanded asset purchase programme (APP) (Working Paper No. 2075). European Central Bank

Hesse H, Hofmann B, Weber J (2017) The macroeconomic effects of asset purchases revisited (Working paper No. 680). Bank for International Settlements

International Monetary Fund (2018a) Global financial stability report, October 2018: a decade after the global financial crisis: are we safer?

International Monetary Fund (2018b) World Economic Outlook, October 2018: challenges to steady growth

Joyce M, Liu Z, Tonks I (2015) Institutional investor investment behavior during the crisis and the portfolio balance effect of QE, VOX CEPR's policy portal, voxeu.org, January 3

Koo RC (2011) The world in balance sheet recession: causes, cure and politics. Real World Econ Rev (58):19–37

Koo RC (2016) The other half of macroeconomics and the three stages of economic development. Real World Econ Rev (75):2–48

Mishkin FS (2018) The economics of money, banking, and financial markets, 11th edn. Pearson, New York

Praet P (2016) Transmission channels of monetary policy in the current environment. Speech presented at the Financial Times Festival of Finance, London, July 1

Quint D, Rabanal P (2017) Should unconventional monetary policies become conventional? (Discussion Paper No. 28/2017). Deutsche Bundesbank

Storz M, Koetter M, Setzer R, Westphal A (2017) Do we want these two to tango? On zombie firms and stressed banks in Europe (Working Paper No. 2104). European Central Bank

Takahashi W (2013) Japanese monetary policy, experience from the lost decades. Int J Bus 18(4):287–306

Thornton DL (2014) QE: is there a portfolio balance effect? Fed Reserve Bank St. Louis Rev 96(1):55–72

Weber A (2018) Markets must prepare for more volatility. Financial Times, January 8

Yellen JT (2017) Inflation, uncertainty, and monetary policy. Speech presented at the 59th annual meeting of the National Association of Business Economists in Cleveland, OH, September 26

# 4

# Side Effects of Monetary Accommodation

**Abstract** The long period of monetary accommodation after the Great Financial Crisis has triggered an intensive debate about the potentially negative side effects of these policies—especially regarding the growth and distribution of financial wealth and the stability of financial market development. Clearly, the interest income of savers has declined as a result of monetary policy in the euro area, while borrowers have benefited. The long-term income to be expected from savings funds, especially for retirement, has diminished, due to the dearth of returns. Therefore, funds need to be replenished. Financial markets have become more exposed to the risk of high asset valuations and—in recent years—to a return of rising leverage in most economies. Such side effects of monetary policy that intend to stimulate economic activity in the short term pose risks for future long-term growth. For the euro area, the ECB's monetary policy has affected countries differently, benefiting economies with higher net borrowing in the private and public sector. Also, the rise of Target II imbalances in the payments system of the ECB shows that there has been a redistribution of sovereign risks in the course of the central bank's asset purchase program.


M. Heise, *Inflation Targeting and Financial Stability*,
https://doi.org/10.1007/978-3-030-05078-8_4

## 4.1 The Impact on Financial Wealth and Retirement Assets

Expansionary monetary policy measures, such as rate cuts and bond purchases, have various effects on the growth of private savings and retirement funds. Rising asset prices will benefit the owners of bonds, equities and real estate. In the years of monetary policy accommodation, financial wealth showed decent rates of return even in the euro area. Actually, as shown in Chap. 3, rising asset valuations accounted for the biggest part of financial wealth growth in the post-crisis period. Rising asset prices helped to compensate for the very low yields on bank accounts and safe bonds (Fig. 4.1).[1] For the euro area (here calculated as an average of the eight largest economies) nominal returns were quite solid in the years after the debt crisis of 2011. Given the rather low inflation in those years, real returns were not significantly lower than during the pre-crisis years.

These statistics—often used in defense of expansionary monetary policies—seem to show that savers have not suffered that much. This verdict might hold true for the last couple of years. The statistics, however, conceal problems stored up for the future. Continuously rising valuations over a broad range of assets—from bonds to equities and real estate—have drastically reduced the return expectations that determine the growth of financial wealth in the future. With benchmark bond yields still close to zero in the eurozone and Japan, bond prices cannot go much higher and investors in these instruments will suffer real losses for the foreseeable future. After the boom years, investors will also have to reduce their return expectations for listed equity, private equity and real estate in many countries.

For private and institutional investors, lower returns on financial assets mean that future income streams will be lower. Retirement savings might no longer be sufficient to achieve aspired income levels. With lower expected returns, savings must actually be increased in order to achieve the same future capital income. How strong the effect from expected returns is can be illustrated in a simple example: With a return of 2%, savings of EUR 500 per month over 20 years will yield a payout of only EUR 147,000, while a return of 5% would generate EUR 203,000. Put differently, if the expected return falls to 2%, but the aspired retirement payout stays at EUR 203,000, the saver would have to increase his or her monthly savings from EUR 500 to EUR 688.

---

[1] Allianz (2017).

*Belgium, Germany, Finland, France, Italy, Netherlands, Austria, Portugal und Spain.

Yields calculation includes all types of bank deposits, securities, pension and insurance claims.

Source: Eurostat, Allianz Research

**Fig. 4.1** Yields on financial assets and inflation in the eurozone

Lower returns require significant adjustments for the providers of long-term income streams, including insurance companies, pension funds and firms that offer defined benefit pension plans for their employees. The liabilities in their balance sheets need to be discounted with a lower interest rate, implying that the present value of these claims rises. Basically, there are three options to adjust. Where possible, depending on the type of pension plan, contribution rates can be increased or future payouts reduced. In defined contribution plans, employees have to expect lower payouts when they retire. Where guarantees have been given, the pension providers need to set aside more capital to cover their future liabilities. In the insurance business, this is required by official capital regulation. Firms that have offered defined benefit pensions to their employees have to fund the resulting deficits. For some companies, these account for a significant share of their balance sheets. Out of 2600 companies covered by one research team, 1075 showed a pension deficit. Taken together, these deficits amount to USD 790 billion.[2]

If one calculates the gap between expected future pensions and the payouts that would be needed for a decent standard of living in retirement (say, 70% of final salaries), the "protection gaps" are even greater.[3] Globally, these gaps add up to roughly USD 40 trillion, based on the gap between the income generated by capital funded pensions plus first-pillar pensions and 70% of final salaries. The gap grows with the decline in interest rates. Such rough calculations show that temporary valuation gains caused by lower interest rates are not the most important part of the picture.

## 4.2 The Impact on Inequality

Monetary policy also has distributional effects. It changes the distribution between savers and borrowers. Expansionary policies lower the interest income of savers and reduce the debt service for borrowers. Over the monetary cycle, these effects should even out. But if accommodative policies become entrenched for a long time, distributional effects can get serious. The other dimension of redistribution is between the holders of risky assets, which deliver valuation gains in times of falling interest rates, and savers, who rely on bank deposits that yield little or nothing in times of expansionary monetary policy.

[2] UBS Global Research, 23. April 2018.

[3] Geneva Association (2018).

In most countries, households with lower income and wealth typically hold a relatively higher share of their money in bank deposits and liquid assets, whereas higher income earners will own relatively more shares, bonds and real estate. Central bank surveys show that in seven of the eight larger euro area countries, the portfolio share of bank deposits is significantly higher for the bottom deciles of the wealth distribution than for the wealthier classes (Fig. 4.2). The exception is the Netherlands, where about 90% of all employees invest in quasi-mandatory occupational pensions that basically consist of securities.

Based on these portfolio shares, it is possible to calculate average nominal returns for the individual deciles of the wealth distribution.[4] As Fig. 4.3 shows, returns were mostly higher for wealthier households, but the difference is not big in all countries. Although the basic message is confirmed—the first-round effect of rising asset prices is to widen inequality—generalizations are nevertheless difficult. The final impact of monetary policy on the wealth distribution depends on a number of other factors, e.g. who benefits from lower costs of credit and the opportunity to refinance debt more cheaply. This, in turn, depends on the level and duration of debt in different income groups as well as on whether fixed or flexible rate contracts are more common in a country. If interest rates are mainly flexible, as e.g. in Spain, the debt service burden quickly goes down when monetary policy lowers short-term interest rates. In countries where long-term fixed rate mortgages play a larger role, as in Germany, lower interest rates will take time to filter through into lower debt servicing costs.

In addition, there is an effect on house prices that is not included in the above return calculation. While higher house prices should, in general, favor wealthier households, the effect can also be strong for less wealthy households in countries where ownership rates and leverage on property are relatively high. Given the interplay of these various factors, it is no surprise that analyses of distributional effects of monetary policy have produced mixed results.[5] A number of studies have even reported positive distributional effects of monetary expansion, under the assumption that these policies effectively help to reduce unemployment.

What can be confirmed, however, is the redistribution between net savers and net borrowers: in countries where households are avid net savers and hold

[4] Allianz (2017).

[5] See, for example, Deutsche Bundesbank (2016), Draghi (2015), El-Herradi (2017), Furceri et al. (2016), Domanski et al. (2016), O'Farrell et al. (2016), and Adam and Tzamourani (2016).

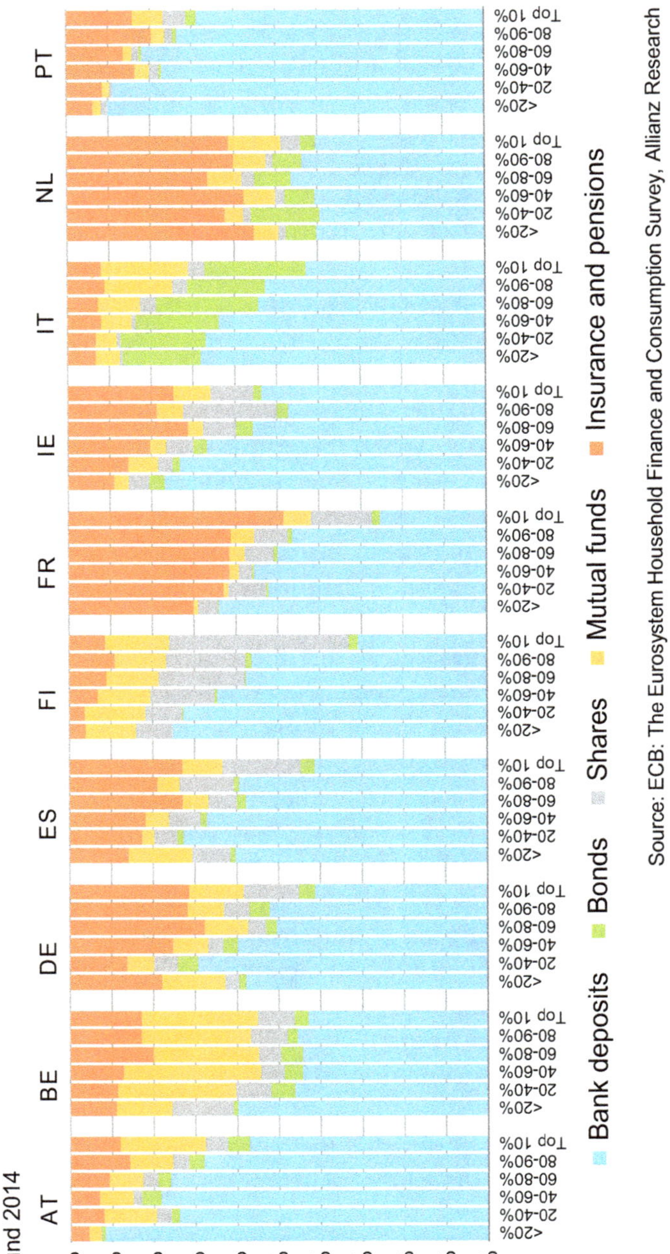


**Fig. 4.2** Portfolio structure by income group

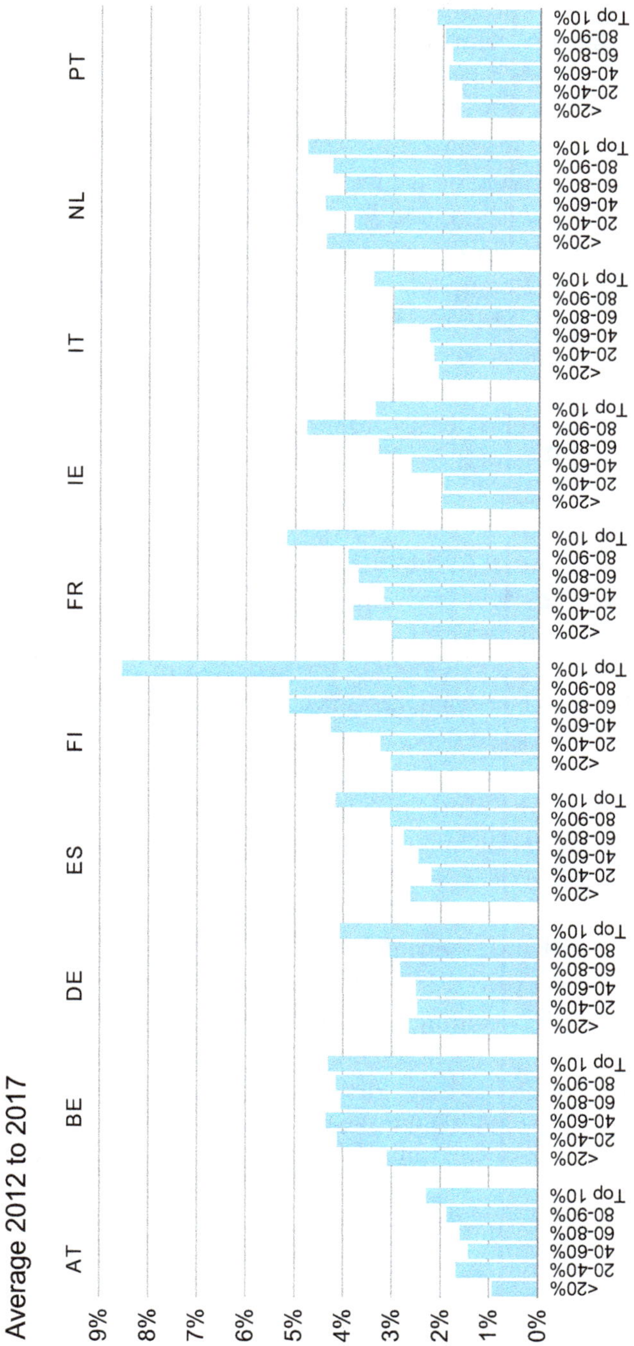


Source: ECB: The Eurosystem Household Finance and Consumption Survey, Allianz Research

**Fig. 4.3** Nominal total return by income group

significant net financial wealth, the impact of lower interest rates will tend to be less favorable than in countries where households have incurred large amounts of debt and hence benefit from lower borrowing costs. This fact can be illustrated by an analysis of the direct impact of monetary policy on incomes in the euro area. The "direct impact on income" refers to net interest rate gains or losses for households as a result of changes in the interest rates on bank deposits, on the one hand, and loans, on the other. In contrast to the effects of monetary policy on the prices of assets such as shares, bonds and receivables from insurance companies and pension funds, which initially represent "only" book profits or losses, households feel these changes directly in their wallets (or their bank accounts).

Comparing interest rate income and payments, private households in the euro area have benefited substantially from the ECB's policy. Since 2012, the year in which the ECB vowed to do "whatever it takes" to save the euro, cumulative interest rate gains have come to EUR 148 billion, or EUR 440 per capita. The extremely expansionary monetary policy has been a blessing for households in some countries in the south of the continent in particular, as it significantly reduced their debt service payments. However, interest rate gains have declined noticeably in recent years. The figures are calculated by comparing interest rates on deposits and loans in the period from 2012 to 2017 with the situation in the years before the crisis from 2003 to 2008. In this calculation, changes in the volume of deposits are corrected for.

An analysis by Allianz Research[6] concludes that the main winners from low interest rates have been the southern euro crisis countries, such as Portugal and Spain. Households in Finland, the Netherlands and France have also generally fared better during the years of low interest rates because of relatively high debt ratios. In "countries of savers", such as Germany, Austria and Belgium, on the other hand, the trend over the last 8 years has been much more negative than in the pre-crisis years, with net interest incomes of Belgian and Austrian households becoming negative (Fig. 4.4).

There is one exception to the observation that low interest rates have mostly benefitted southern countries: Italy. First, Italian households are not highly indebted and second, they stand out due to their particular investment behavior. In Italy, households hold more bonds privately than those anywhere else in the euro area.

[6] Allianz (2018).

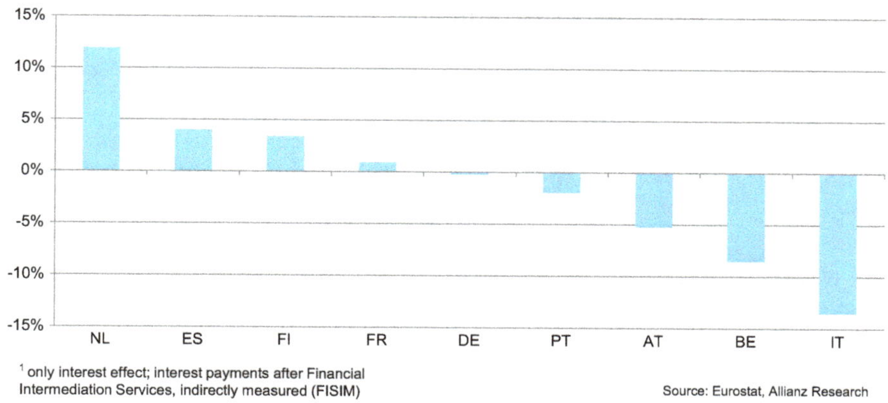


**Fig. 4.4** Cumulated changes in net interest income between 2008 and 2016 as percent of GDP

## 4.3 Target II Imbalances

One much-discussed side effect of monetary policy in the euro area has been the emergence of significant intra-euro area imbalances in central banks' payment system (Target II). Critics claim that the Target II imbalances are tantamount to invisible credit lines between member countries and a form of risk sharing through the back door. They have triggered a lengthy debate about whether the ECB's asset purchase programs are in compliance with EU treaties (especially Article 123, which prohibits monetary financing of state deficits). Among the issues discussed have been whether purchases of government bonds on secondary markets constitute monetary financing of public debt and whether the potentially unlimited purchases through the OMT program contravene the no-bailout clause of EU treaties. Whatever legal positions one might take on these issues, it seems clear that economically there has to some extent been a redistribution of risks between the countries of the currency union.[7] A major factor has been the build-up of Target II imbalances (Fig. 4.5).

Target II is the payments system for bank transactions run by the Eurosystem of central banks. Claims or liabilities that central banks accumulate in the Target system are integrated into international payments accounting and are part of a country's net foreign asset position, although they are not legally enforceable claims between countries. Target (im)balances arise when either net exports or net capital flows between countries are financed through the

[7] Sinn (2018), see also Sinn (2014).

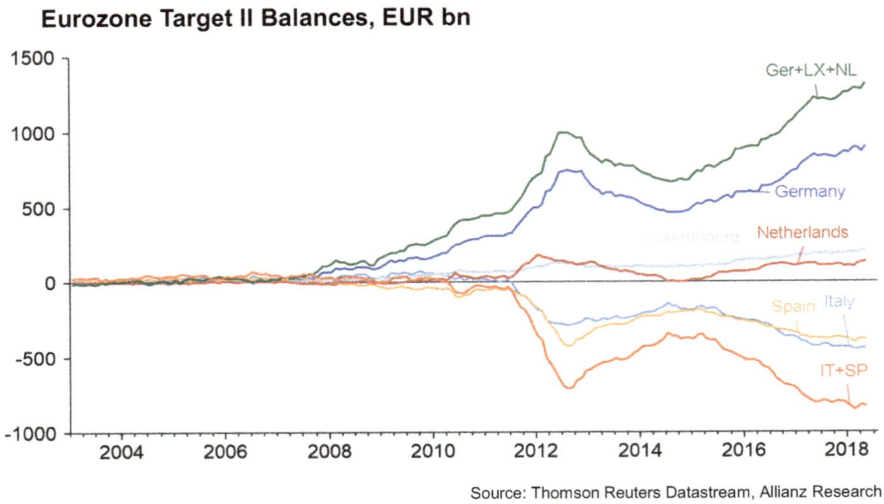


**Fig. 4.5** Target II (im)balances rise to ever higher levels

system of central banks. During the debt crisis, when capital fled countries such as Greece, Italy, Spain, Ireland and Portugal, Target was vital for the survival of the Eurosystem. Commercial banks in these countries received the liquidity they needed from their national central banks, not via interbank loans as in pre-crisis times. Unlimited funding from central banks alleviated the liquidity constraints.

However, the expectation that Target II imbalances would largely disappear once the debt crisis subsided has not been fulfilled. Imbalances shrank in the years after Mario Draghi's "whatever it takes" speech, which reestablished confidence that the currency union would not disintegrate. Since the start of Quantitative Easing with the APP program, however, imbalances have widened again. Central bank purchases of government and corporate bonds created international payments flows that led to increasingly negative balances for Italy and Spain. The reason is that the central banks of these countries purchased bonds through banks outside of their borders. For example, if the Banca d'Italia purchased an Italian government bond from a bank or an investor in Frankfurt, the transaction would lead to a claim of the Banca d'Italia vis-a-vis the Italian government and a Target II liability vis-a-vis the Deutsche Bundesbank. The Bundesbank, in turn, is liable for the deposit of the bank that sold the bonds. As a result of such a transaction, a foreign held claim on the Italian government has been substituted by a claim of the Italian central bank on its own government, while the selling institution has a claim in its national banking system. If the seller of the bond in Frankfurt were to transfer the liquidity earned by the asset sale to a bank in Italy, this would reduce the Target II liabilities of the Banca d'Italia. Such transfers, however, do not seem to have taken place on a significant scale. So, while the Asset Purchase program of the ECB was designed to be symmetrical, in the sense that bonds of each country are purchased in an amount related to its economic size (the capital key of the ECB), the outcome is not symmetrical if Target II imbalances are taken into account.

In the end, persistent Target II imbalances are a sign that the cross-border money market for banks is still dysfunctional. The total amount of cross-border bank lending, which includes money market transactions, has declined by no less than 1300 billion within the euro area since 2008 (Fig. 4.6).

The financing of a large part of net exports or net capital flows between countries has been transferred to the public sector. The fact that the central banks in the euro area provide as much liquidity as needed at zero cost is a strong incentive for banks to refinance via central banks and not via credit lines from other banks or bank bonds. If monetary policy were to end its strategy of "full allotment" and limit the amount of central bank money, banks would return to the money market to cover their liquidity yields. Such

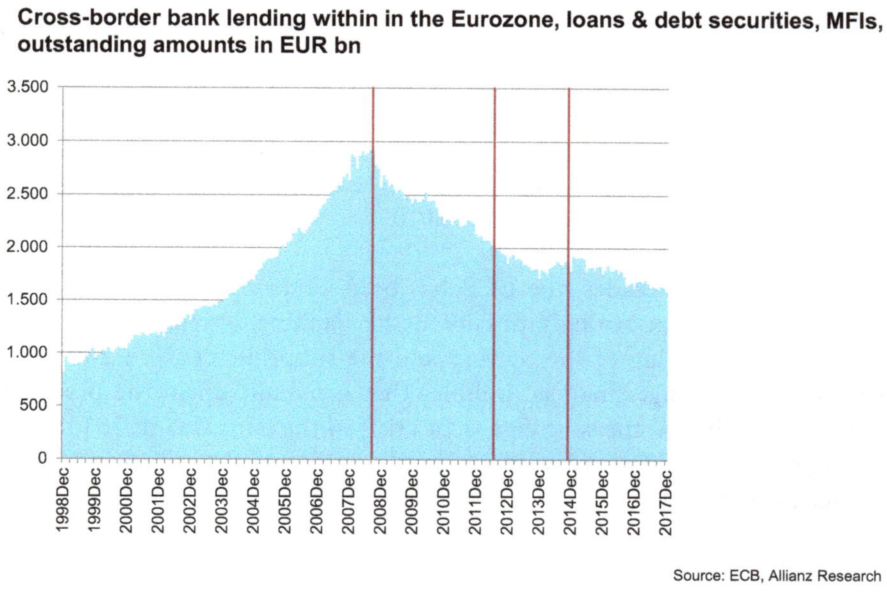


**Fig. 4.6** Inter-bank lending squeeze in the eurozone

a normalization of monetary policy would certainly reduce target imbalances again. It would most likely be more effective than other proposals that have been made like, for example, charging positive interest rates on target liabilities (presently no interest payments are charged, as the relevant central rate of the ECB is zero) or introducing safety deposits in the form of gold or other international reserves. Such measures would affect the relationship amongst the central banks, but would not alter the incentives for commercial banks to use central bank funding for cross-border transactions in the first place.

Additionally, further steps to integrate the banking systems in the euro area would most likely reduce payments imbalances. In the US, significant payments imbalances between the districts of the Fed can arise, but they are much smaller than in the euro area. This is not only due to rebalancing requirements, but also to the fact that the USA's banking system is fully integrated, since major banks operate nationwide and balance payments within their organization. If the euro area also had more truly pan-European banks, Target II imbalances would not be as big an issue. Target II imbalances are, therefore, another urgent reason to make progress on the Banking Union.

## 4.4 The Risk of Serial Financial Bubbles

> According to a database compiled at the IMF, 147 individual national banking crises occurred between 1970 and 2011. They were colossally expensive, in terms of lost output, increased public debt and, not least, political credibility. Within just 3 years from 2007, cumulative output losses, relative to trend, were 31% of gross domestic product in the US. In the UK, the recent crisis imposed a fiscal cost only exceeded by the Napoleonic war and the two world wars. Martin Wolf, Financial Times, June 6, 2018.

In the last two decades, the ECB has been confronted with three major economic crises that strongly disrupted the banking system. The dot.com crisis at the beginning of the century and the subprime crisis in 2008 were both a result of huge financial bubbles that had built up in the preceding boom years, whereas the sovereign debt crisis in the euro area in 2011–2012 reflected widespread fears of sovereign insolvencies fueled by the restructuring of Greek debt.[8]

---

[8] For an analysis see Heise (2013, Chap. 3).

These various crises have undermined the confidence in the financial system. As markets gyrated and confidence collapsed, huge amounts of wealth were destroyed, output was lost and unemployment rose in many places. During the great financial crisis of 2008, the financial system ceased to fulfill its function as bank funding completely dried out.

While the recession after the tech-boom in 1999 was fairly light, given the huge losses of wealth it had created, the crisis that followed the subprime boom destroyed millions of jobs and billions in income. Growth rates have normalized in the years since, but losses in the levels of production and income have remained. This has been reflected by the debates about secular stagnation or L-shaped adjustment paths. "Indeed, empirical evidence indicates that many recessions, especially those that coincide with banking crises, have permanent effects on output—growth may return to its pre-crisis long-term trend, but output does not, so that a permanent gap develops between the pre- and post-recession output trends" Mikael Juselius et al., page 2 BIS July 2016.

The prevailing concept of inflation targeting does not foresee mitigation of financial cycles as a central role of monetary policy. Correspondingly, in recent decades, central banks have not pursued a strategy of "leaning against the wind" of financial markets. Policies have been calibrated with respect to inflation targets. As inflation was rather moderate before the subprime crisis, there seemed to be no need for more restrictive policies. Also, in the years since the Great Financial Crisis, inflation has remained low (often below target), allowing monetary authorities to continue their accommodative policies for a long time despite increasing risks in financial markets. Policy makers justify their focus on consumer price inflation with the argument that save-guarding consumers' purchasing power should their main objective. Furthermore, they do not see inflation targets as a one-dimensional policy design. Rather, they assume that price stability is a pre-condition for stable growth and employment, and, in the past, also saw it as a necessary (but not sufficient) condition for financial stability. The latter assumption—that price stability and financial stability go hand in hand—has, however, not stood up to the test of reality in the Great Financial Crisis.

For many years, the US Fed followed what has become known as the "Greenspan" doctrine. It says that the costs of mopping up the damages wrought by a financial bubble are likely to be smaller than the losses in terms of growth and employment that result from the attempt to prevent a bubble through preemptive interest rates hikes. Fed policy has reflected this doctrine. In the late 1990s, when the tech boom accelerated, the Fed did little to stop it. It slightly reduced the Fed Funds rate to 4.7% at the end of 1998, when market exaggerations were already apparent. It then hiked the rate up to 6.5% in November 2000. As Alan Greenspan pointed out, however, this did not significantly push up bond yields (Fig. 4.7) and, therefore, did not clearly dampen the financial upswing. This was not seen as a big problem, as the tech-boom was expected to increase the flexibility of supply and raise potential output, thus dampening consumer prices. With hindsight we know that there was no acceleration of potential output. The economic cycle was alive, and the financial boom was followed by a serious bust that was reinforced by the terrorist attacks on the World Trade Center in 2001. The market crash in 2000 corrected the overvaluation of stocks caused by "irrational exuberance". Central banks were left with the job of clearing up the rubble and limiting the damage. By 2004, the Fed had decreased the Fed Funds rate to around 1%.

At that point, a new financial cycle had already started and was gaining speed. Rising leverage in the private sector and massive speculation in the real estate sector followed. The Fed hiked rates in 2005 and 2006 and held them on a plateau of around 5% from mid-2006 to mid-2007. Again, the effect on

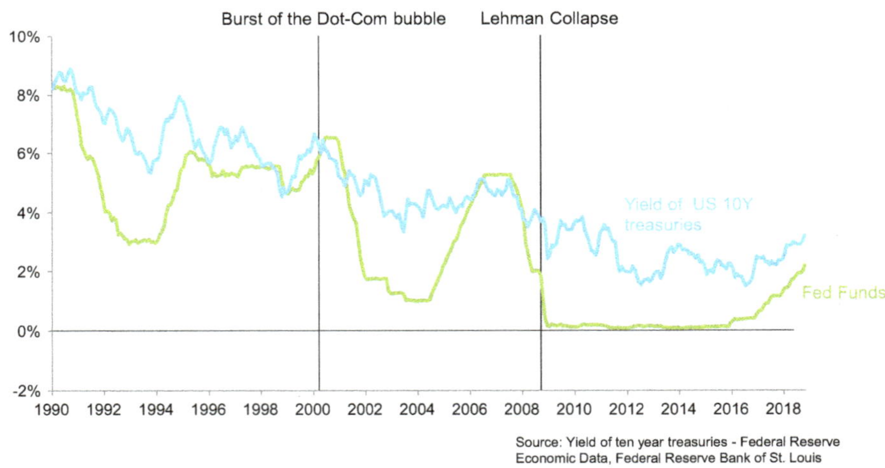


**Fig. 4.7** Fed policy and the cycle

long-term yields was rather weak, creating the Greenspan conundrum already mentioned in Chap. 2. The speculative boom kept growing until there were first signs that the bubble was bursting in the second half of 2007. With the failure of two of Bear Stearns' hedge funds in March 2008 and the collapse of Lehmann Brothers in September 2008, the Fed quickly and aggressively cut its interest rate to almost zero in 2009 and became the lender of last resort for the banking system. Financial markets stabilized in 2009 and notched up significant gains in the years thereafter. But the Fed and other central banks kept interest rates close to zero and resorted to large-scale asset purchases. After successful crisis resolution, they then started fighting low growth and low inflation in the post-crisis years.

Given the enormous economic and social costs of financial crises, government policy makers and central bankers should find ways to dampen financial market cycles and prevent the violent swings that are part of the boom-bust cycle. Risks always build up in good times, as the IMF reminded us in its 2017 Global Financial Stability Report: "The findings underscore the importance of policymakers maintaining heightened vigilance regarding risks to growth during periods of benign financial conditions that may provide a fertile breeding ground for the accumulation of financial vulnerabilities."[9]

Policy makers' track record of smoothing financial cycles has been miserable in the last two decades. Central banks have argued that detecting financial market mispricing is difficult and that their instruments have their limits when it comes to correcting overshooting markets (see Chap. 5). While these are difficult issues, there are important lessons to be learnt from the crises of the last two decades. We do know that money and credit developments have a strong and leading influence on the financial cycle. Monetary policy matters because it influences these developments. Central bankers should try to dampen, or at least not amplify, financial cycles by aggressively cutting interest rates in periods of downward market corrections and hiking rates only moderately when markets are buoyant. Such asymmetrical policies impart a downward bias to interest rates and incentivize risk taking, as market participants rely on central banks offering "protection" against volatility, and, in the long-run, induce higher leverage in the system. The fact that, for many decades, the long-term growth of credit volumes in advanced economies has been outpacing nominal growth of GDP (see Sect. 4.4) is at least in part a reflection of such policies. Also, at the time of writing, the already high credit-to-GDP ratios are continuing to increase. This rising ratio makes it ever more

[9] IMF (2017, p. 91), see also IMF (2018b, c).

difficult to hike rates, as credit contraction can seriously damage the economy.

To sum up, an economy's exposure to financial risk is the most serious side-effect of central banks keeping monetary policy loose for a long time while consumer price inflation remains below a narrowly defined inflation target. After the Great Financial Crisis, the attempt to use strong and extended monetary accommodation to clean up the damage from the bubble failed. Meanwhile, it has increased financial imbalances, excessive risk taking and leverage. One financial bubble may thus be the breeding ground for the next one. This specter of serial financial bubbles should make central banks include considerations of financial market cycles more firmly in their policies (see Chap. 5).

> These considerations highlight the possibility that, in more ways than one, over long horizons low interest rates may become, to some extent, self-validating. Low rates may beget lower rates as monetary policy contributes to financial booms and busts. Juselius et al. (2016, p. 28).

## 4.5 The Relentless Rise of Debt

In times of growth and positive business sentiment, financial markets typically cheer lending growth. Private lending is seen to herald further growth of demand and production, especially when the "credit impulse", that is the growth rate of new lending (the second derivative of the volume of overall credit), is strong. After years of strong credit impulses, overall private debt levels have reached record highs globally. Combined with high levels of public borrowing, these high levels have become one of the most intractable problems of the global economy.[10] According to the Bank for International Settlements, private debt among non-financial companies plus public debt now amounts to 240% of global GDP (Fig. 4.8). Before the financial crisis, this ratio stood at 210%, and at the end of 2001 at around 190%. Despite strong economic growth in many areas of the world public deficits are still high, most notably in the US, where net public borrowing was set to reach 4.5 % of GDP in 2018, pushing its total public debt to around 108% of GDP. In the euro area, public debt stands at 90% of GDP, a high level, but one that is

[10] Heise (2018).

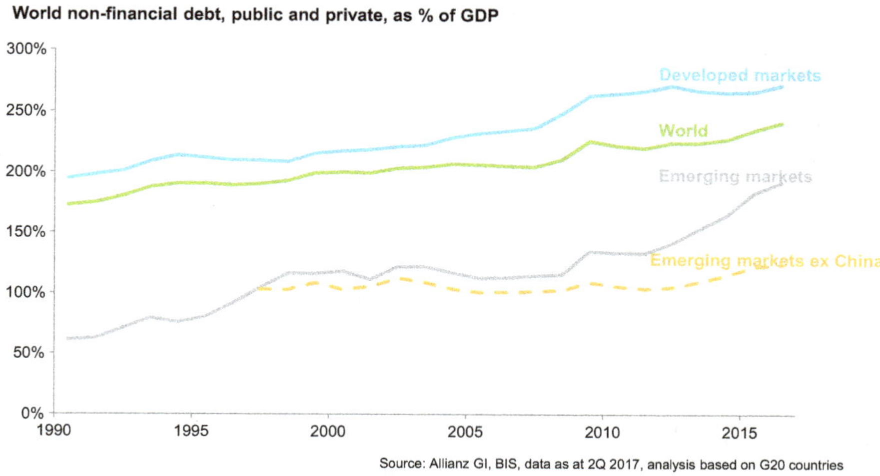


**Fig. 4.8** Deleveraging. What deleveraging?

dwarfed by Japan's (240 %). Globally, private non-financial debt is outpacing nominal growth. The years of post-crisis de-leveraging with a reduction of private debt relative to GDP are over. We are back in an expansionary credit cycle.

How does this return of expanding credit relate to monetary policy? The world's major central banks strongly welcomed the return of lending growth after the period of de-leveraging in which monetary policy instruments did not have much of an impact. Now that western economies have entered a new credit cycle, only the US Fed and the People's Bank of China are taking careful steps to rein in credit growth. The ECB and the Bank of Japan, on the other hand, are still seeking to stimulate credit-financed growth.

High and rising indebtedness is a big risk for western economies. When economies fall into recession with a high level of debt, job losses and income shortfalls can be more severe than would otherwise be the case. During a recession, an increasing amount of loans will become non-performing, forcing banks to write them off. The assets that borrowers have used as collateral will be impaired. Big balance sheet losses will emerge as assets devalue while the amount of nominal debt is largely fixed. Balance sheets have to be repaired by measures of de-risking and de-leveraging, which further reduces aggregate demand. Making things worse, a highly indebted government can do little to help in such a situation. The crisis will damage the government's financial credibility and raise its borrowing costs on the markets. The euro crisis has confirmed that highly indebted governments have little room for anti-cyclical policies. Governments may be forced to start saving in the midst of an economic contraction to maintain access to capital market funding.

To minimize such risks, policy makers and their economic advisors should heed three lessons. Firstly, they need to discard the idea that more debt always leads to more growth. There are certainly times when governments need to borrow to stimulate the economy; but deficit spending cannot lift growth in the long run. Governments should have used the positive growth environment of recent years to reduce their own deficits more strongly, especially as the private sector has been borrowing again. The EU, for example, has recently seen its strongest growth in decades whilst private credit demand has been rising. In such an environment, all countries should have been able to meet the fiscal criteria of the Stability and Growth Pact. The tendency of some governments to avoid fiscal consolidation even in good times and instead lambast it as "austerity" will exacerbate the economic and financial cycle.

Secondly, the best way to avoid unsustainable debt is for a country to stimulate long-term, non-debt financed growth. Regulation, trade agreements, investment incentives as well as labor market and educational reforms are part of a government's toolbox in this endeavor. Central banks can support the impact of such reforms through expansionary monetary policies, though they should calibrate their instruments carefully. Once economies have moved out of a balance sheet crisis and lending has recovered, as we have been observing for some years, monetary policy should not focus on pushing up leverage in the private sector further. Negative deposit rates, designed to pressure banks to lend more, or liquidity operations that are conditional on bank lending levels, are questionable in this environment. Instead, central banks should continue to employ forward guidance to influence interest rate expectations and bond yields. If deemed necessary, such forward guidance and yield management will fuel asset price increases and stimulate demand in a whole range of areas, not only through higher corporate leverage. Having said that, asset prices are already high and economies are growing healthily at the time of writing. Therefore, central banks should follow the Fed in gradually reducing their stimulus.

Thirdly, and crucially, regulators need to create a market framework that ensures efficient capital allocation where private debt is channeled into productive uses that offer decent longer-term returns. The "subprime" crisis is probably the best example of a situation in which this target was completely missed. Such failures put the spotlight on regulatory policies designed to prevent excessive risk taking and market overheating, so-called macro-prudential policies. Their mission is to tighten regulation in segments of financial markets where major risks are building up and create buffers in times of market down-

| | |
|---|---|
| 1 | **Repricing of risk premia in global financial markets**<br>Vulnerabilities: mispricing of risks and excessive risk-taking amid a historically low cost of funding/low returns on savings and a search for yield by financial investors<br>Potential triggers: shocks to risk-free rates (such as monetary policy developments in main currency areas, inflation or fiscal shocks) or to risk premia (for example, as a result of geopolitical events or the materialisation of vulnerabilities in key emerging market economies) |
| 2 | **Persistent weaknesses in the balance sheets of banks, insurers and pension schemes**<br>Vulnerabilities (banks): challenges to sustainable sources of profit in the low interest rate environment with structural changes like digitalisation and fintech challenging banks' businesses, significant asset quality issues still persist in certain countries<br>Vulnerabilities (life insurers and pension schemes): low-yield environment increasing the liabilities of life insurers and pension schemes and creating return challenges for long-term investments in high-quality assets<br>Potential triggers: significant prolonged profitability pressures (banks), revaluation of liabilities at low interest rates (life insurers), weak returns on financial investments, materialisation of system-wide cyber risk |
| 3 | **Debt sustainability challenges in the sovereign, corporate and household sectors**<br>Vulnerabilities: high indebtedness in public and/or private sectors, as well as limited fiscal space to absorb shocks<br>Potential triggers: materialisation of political risks, repricing in financial markets, unsustainable fiscal spending, shocks to the medium-term growth outlook arising from the slow implementation of structural reforms |
| 4 | **Vulnerabilities in the shadow banking system and contagion to the wider financial system**<br>Vulnerabilities: rapidly increasing size and complexity of the shadow banking system, liquidity and leverage risks among certain types of investment funds, interconnectedness and risk of contagion to other parts of the financial system, including through cross-border linkages, a lack of transparency and of data for comprehensive risk monitoring<br>Potential triggers: repricing in global financial markets, with a potential for fire sales and liquidity squeezes |

Source: ESRB Annual Report 2017, European Systemic Risk Board

**Fig. 4.9** Overview of the main risks to financial stability in the EU

turns. At the time of writing, the main types of risk for EU financial markets can be seen in Fig. 4.9, which is taken from the 2018 annual report of the European Systemic Risk Board (ESRB),[11] the euro area's macro-prudential watchdog.

Paul Tucker, the former deputy governor of the Bank of England, explains the role of macro-prudential policy as follows: "micro-prudential supervision and macro-prudential policy overlap in all sorts of ways. They share an objective; and macro-prudential instruments are simply micro-regulatory requirements calibrated to the needs of the system as a whole".[12] Important measures in this respect have been the introduction of anti-cyclical capital buffers in the Basel III agreement as well as supplementary capital buffers for systemic risks and systemically relevant financial institutions.

As macro-prudential policy measures are linked to proxies of the financial cycle, an understanding of these cycles, and their manifestations, causes and implications is important for policy makers.[13] For example, counter-cyclical capital buffers are linked to deviations in the credit-to-GDP ratio from its long-run trend. Capital should be accumulated when systemic risk is increasing, creating buffers that support the resilience of the banking sector during periods of stress when losses materialize. This will help maintain the supply of credit and dampen the downswing in the financial cycle. But as the IMF reports in its recent Global Financial Stability Report, the main counter-cyclical capital tool, the counter-cyclical capital buffer, has been used rather infrequently. At the end of 2017, most jurisdictions of the Basel Committee on Banking Supervision had not set the counter-cyclical capital buffer above zero, despite strong credit growth and the emergence of large credit gaps. In countries that do not apply the rules of the Basel Committee, the use of counter-cyclical capital buffers has been sparing. According to the IMF the reasons vary: "some country authorities feel that risks can be sufficiently contained with other tools, either microprudential or macroprudential, or that taking into account other indicators of credit risk would weigh against its (the counter-cyclical buffers) use. Others are concerned that activating counter-cyclical capital buffer will lead to disintermediation as bank costs rise above those of less regulated sectors" (IMF GFSR 2018a, p. 62). More common macro-prudential measures are restrictions on bank lending to households. For example, changes to the maximum loan-to-value or loan-to-income ratios that apply to

[11] ESRB (2018), see also ESRB (2016, 2017).

[12] Tucker (2017, p. 333).

[13] Kunovac et al. (2018).

mortgage borrowers and restrictions on the eligibility of borrowers can help to constrain or stimulate mortgage markets. Whether such instruments will actually help to smooth real estate and mortgage cycles in the future remains to be seen. As shown in Sect. 3.2, major real estate markets have been booming in recent years of expansionary monetary policies and prices in some regions have skyrocketed. As real estate property accounts for a large share of overall wealth and is widely used as collateral for lending, this is a risk for financial stability.

As a conclusion, one may argue that the strengthening of macro-prudential regulation is an important supplement and innovation to the toolbox of regulatory and supervisory policies. But its impact in terms of smoothing cycles and sustaining financial stability is likely to be moderate as long as loose monetary conditions incentivize risk taking by market participants. The institutions that propose macro-prudential policies have limited power of enforcement. In the euro area, for example, the ESRB publishes recommendations to national regulators but does not implement regulations itself. National regulators can decide to add regulations for macro-prudential reasons, although those often meet objections by the affected industry, as such add-on regulations influence the competitive position of the industry and often challenge the viability of its business models. Therefore, they have been and probably will be implemented in a measured way.

Coming back to the bigger picture, it seems fair to say that governments, regulators and central banks will always face difficult choices in their attempts to prevent the build-up of large financial risks. Monetary tightening may weaken growth and derail markets, at least temporarily. Macro-prudential measures can mitigate the financial risks of extended periods of ultra-low interest rates, but they cannot completely counteract their effects. Finally, the kind of structural reforms needed to move an economy away from debt-fueled growth are hardly ever popular. In the current febrile political environment, none of this will be easy to implement. But what happens if governments and monetary authorities avoid such hard choices? We might see a repeat of recent history. The financial cycle will gain full force, sooner or later asset prices will massively overshoot, leverage ratios will rise further from already high levels, and demand will outstrip capacity, thus causing inflation. The going will be good as long as no external shocks hit our economies and central banks keep their foot on the accelerator. But as evidence of exuberance mounts and inflation picks up, central banks will be forced to change course. Financial markets—driven up by low interest rates and ample liquidity—would take a hit. Private leverage and public debt levels would suddenly be seen as unsustainable. Hard and pro-cyclical adjustments would follow. Chapter 5 discusses how monetary policy could incorporate such financial dynamics more explicitly.

## References

Adam K, Tzamourani P (2016) Distributional consequences of asset price inflation in the euro area. Eur Econ Rev 89:172–192

Allianz (2017) Brandmeir K, Holzhausen A. Returns on private assets in selected EMU countries (Working Paper No. 211)

Allianz (2018) Brandmeir K, Holzhausen A. The net interest income of private households (Working Paper No. 212)

Deutsche Bundesbank (2016) Distributional effects of monetary policy. Monthly Report September 2016, 68(9)

Domanski D, Scatigna M, Zabai A (2016) Wealth inequality and monetary policy. BIS Quarterly Review, March 2016

Draghi M (2015) The ECB's recent monetary policy measures, effectiveness and challenges. Lecture presented at the Camdessus Lecture of the IMF in Washington, DC on May 14

El-Herradi M (2017) The redistributive impacts of ECB's unconventional monetary policies: evidence from Italian household surveys. Phd Thesis (Working Paper). University of Bordeaux

ESRB (2016) European Systemic Risk Board. Macroprudential policy issues arising from low interest rates and structural changes in the EU financial system

ESRB (2017) European Systemic Risk Board. Annual report 2016

ESRB (2018) European Systemic Risk Board. Annual report 2017

Furceri D, Loungani P, Zdzienicka A (2016) The effects of monetary policy shocks on inequality (Working Paper No. 16/245). IMF.

Geneva Association (2018) Schanz K. Research brief: understanding and addressing the global insurance protection gaps

Heise M (2013) Emerging from the Euro debt crisis: making the single currency work. Springer, Berlin

Heise M (2018) The debt shackles return. Project Syndicate, May 15

International Monetary Fund (2017) Global financial stability report, October 2017: is growth at risk?

International Monetary Fund (2018a) Global financial stability report, October 2018: a decade after the global financial crisis: are we safer?

International Monetary Fund (2018b) Global financial stability report, April 2018: a bumpy road ahead

International Monetary Fund (2018c) World Economic Outlook, April 2018: cyclical upswing, structural change

Juselius M, Borio C, Disyatat P, Drehmann M (2016) Monetary policy, the financial cycle and ultra-low interest rates (Working Paper No. 569). Monetary and Economic Department, BIS.

Kunovac D, Mandler M, Scharnagl M (2018) Financial cycles in euro area economies: a cross-country perspective (Deutsche Bundesbank Discussion Paper No. 04/2018)

O'Farrell R, Rawdanowicz L, Inaba K (2016) Monetary policy and inequality (Working Paper No. 1281). OECD

Robinson G, Weyns G, Billfalk-Kelly I, Kelly C, Urwin J (2018) Could there be an upside to a pension deficit? UBS Global Research

Sinn HW (2014) The Euro Trap: on bursting bubbles, budgets, and beliefs. Oxford University Press, Oxford

Sinn HW (2018) The ECB's Fiscal Policy (CESifo Working Paper No. 7019). Munich Society for the Promotion of Economic Research—CESifo GmbH

Tucker P (2017) Central banks as trustees for monetary system stability: combining banking supervision with monetary policy. In: ECB legal conference 2017

Wolf M (2018) Why the Swiss should vote for 'Vollgeld'. Financial Times, June 6

# 5

# Towards a Monetary Policy Fit for the Future

*One cannot look back at the Great Moderation today without asking whether the sustained economic stability of the period somehow promoted the excessive risk-taking that followed. The idea that this long period of relative calm lulled investors, financial firms, and financial regulators into paying insufficient attention to risks that were accumulating must have some truth in it. I don't think we should conclude, though, that we therefore should not strive to achieve economic stability. Rather, the right conclusion is that, even in (or perhaps, especially in) stable and prosperous times, monetary policymakers and financial regulators should regard safeguarding financial stability to be of equal importance as—indeed, a necessary prerequisite for—maintaining macroeconomic stability.*
(Bernanke 2013, p. 10)

**Abstract** Clear rules have their advantages. But the enthusiasm for simple inflation targets as the main principle of monetary policy has waned after the crisis, as various central banks consistently missed their targets despite ultra-expansive policies. Meanwhile, the crisis once again supplied evidence of the painful consequences that financial market instability can have for economic growth and social stability. Central banks, including the ECB, should take the side-effects of their policies on financial stability more explicitly into account. Globalization and technological change have affected the way prices and wages are determined. The ensuing uncertainty has strengthened the case for a more adaptable strategy of inflation targeting. Such a strategy should leave room for central banks to systematically smooth the financial cycle, leaning against the wind in times of financial booms and loosening financial condi-


M. Heise, *Inflation Targeting and Financial Stability*,
https://doi.org/10.1007/978-3-030-05078-8_5

tions in times of volatility. Such a policy would improve the long-term performance of the economy.

## 5.1 Recalibrating Inflation Targets

According to Otmar Issing, the first chief economist of the ECB, "In the early 1990s, when the statute of the future European Central Bank was discussed, there was a broad consensus about the optimal framework for a central bank:

1. Price stability should be the objective.
2. Political independence would allow the central bank to conduct the right monetary policy to reach this goal.

The ensuing Great Moderation, a period of low and stable inflation, satisfactory results for growth and employment, seemed to support this view. Financial stability concerns were largely ignored. It was assumed that maintaining price stability would, more or less, implicitly also guarantee financial stability. (…) However, "maintaining price stability is not enough", was a major lesson from the 2008/2009 financial crisis…." Issing (2017, p. 340).

The question is: how can financial stability and price stability be reconciled in a monetary policy strategy? This question has been subject of contentious debate among policy makers and experts. The topic is not new, but once again gaining relevance, as the financial cycle is in full swing and policy makers have few defenses left if and when the cycle starts turning downwards. Central banks could start by defining price stability targets (whether explicit or implicit) in a more adaptable way. They have essentially three options for doing this.[1]

First, they could extend the number of years in which their inflation targets must be reached. Presently, the ECB's communication and inflation projections suggest that the bank operates on a 2–3 year horizon for reaching its price stability target. If the ECB prolonged this period, it could deviate from the reference value for consumer price inflation for a longer time if necessary.

Secondly, central banks could define ranges of inflation that are more easily compatible with price stability. Early adopters of inflation targeting, notably

[1] These and other practical issues of inflation targeting have been discussed since the early days of inflation targeting. See: Bernanke et al. (1999).

the central banks of New Zealand and Canada, have defined a range for inflation of 1 to 3% in the medium term.[2] Similarly, the Bank of Australia has been pursuing a flexible inflation targeting strategy of around 2–3% for about 25 years.[3] Such ranges give monetary policy more room for maneuver in times of major uncertainty concerning underlying inflationary trends or the possible impact and side-effects of monetary policy.

The gain in terms of flexibility is, nevertheless, very limited. Once the rates of inflation move out of the defined band, central banks are under high pressure to act. If a central bank accepted that inflation stayed outside its target range for longer time periods, its guidance on inflation expectations for market participants would diminish. Therefore, central banks that apply wider inflation targets have an incentive to act forcefully whenever their ranges are missed. Whether such action is warranted depends on the causes for the over-or undershooting. A central bank may be justified in tolerating inflation outside its target range, in, for example, periods of large commodity price swings or strong supply shocks to the economy.

Therefore, a third option may be to more broadly define the target of protecting monetary stability. Axel Weber, formerly member of the ECB's Governing Council, criticizes the narrow focus on consumer prices: "economists now understand inflation as a rise in consumer prices, not as a decline in the value of money resulting from an excessive increase in the money supply. Making matters worse, central banks routinely deny responsibility for any prices other than consumer prices, ignoring that the value of money is reflected in *all* prices, including commodities, real estate, stocks, bonds, and, perhaps most important, exchange rates."[4]

A first, albeit still incomplete, recognition of these arguments would be to widen the definition of price stability targets and move the focus away from a simple year-on-year target for consumer price inflation. There are various reasons why consumer prices do not measure purchasing power as precisely as many people assume:

[2] The paradigm of inflation targeting has changed over time: "At the time targeting was developed, it was seen as a way to bring inflation down. 25 years ago, it was difficult to imagine an environment in which the price level would remain so subdued for so long. But that is where we are today, and the situation is stressing the architecture of monetary policy", Tannenbaum (2018, p. 7).

[3] McKibbin and Panton (2018).

[4] Weber (2015).

- Changes in product quality can only be partially adjusted by hedonic pricing models;
- Economic activity is shifting into services, where prices are inherently more difficult to measure;
- Weights in consumption baskets change when relative prices change, and some products, such as owner-occupied housing, are often not included at all;
- Volatile prices for energy or agricultural products have a strong impact on the year-on-year changes in the cost of living, while not being directly under the control of monetary authorities;
- Price statistics do not include the consumer rent that is generated by the proliferation of free-to-use digital service products.

One way of taking measurement errors into account and thereby making inflation targeting more adaptable would be to build a broader index of price stability. Such an index could be calculated by compounding the rate of change of headline consumer prices, core consumer prices that exclude volatile energy and food components and inflation expectations. All these variables play an essential role in the day-to-day analyses of central banks.

A combined inflation measure with equal weights for the year-on-year change in the Harmonized Consumer Price Index (HCPI), core consumer prices, and inflation expectations as measured by the 5-year inflation swap rate yields a much less volatile index of inflation, as shown in Fig. 5.1. Deviations of such an index from the ECB's reference value of "below, but close to 2%" are much less pronounced than those of the year-on-year change in headline inflation rates. Based on this broader measure, there would have been far less pressure on the ECB to take radical measures to close a perceived deflationary gap during the years of "lowflation". True, communicating a monetary policy based on such a combined inflation measure may require more effort than one based on a single, simple number. However, this does not necessarily mean that there would be less trust in the stability orientation of the central bank. Not only academics are aware of the problems entailed in measuring price changes accurately; the general public is, too. Many people are wondering, for example, why central banks are not limiting the inflation in housing rents or real estate prices and why they are not putting more weight on daily-use products that dominate people's perceptions of inflation. In short, the consumer price index is not universally accepted as a measure of purchasing power. Central banks may enhance their credibility by using a target definition with different elements of price development. If this high-

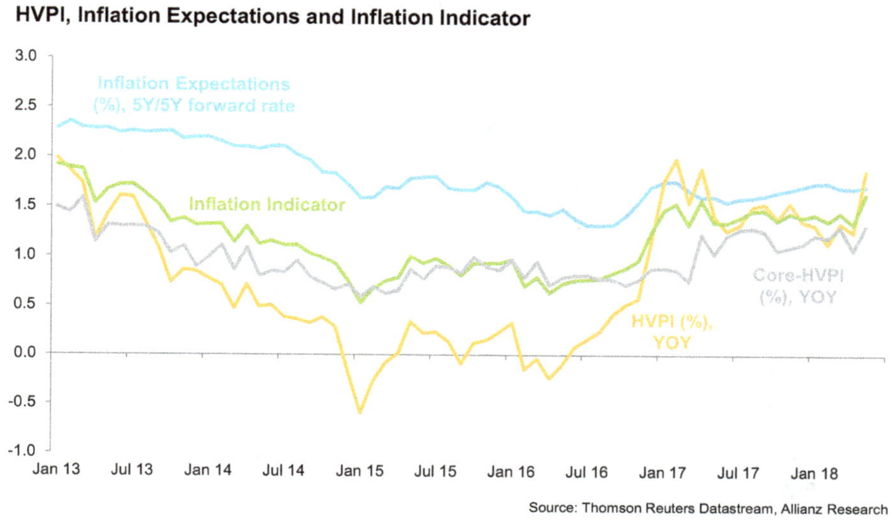


**Fig. 5.1** Suggestion for an inflation indicator

lights that monetary policy is a complicated matter, it may even deepen trust in the ability and determination of central banks to protect the long-term purchasing power of nominal incomes.

The combined index shown in Fig. 5.1 does not address the issue of asset price inflation, though, as highlighted by Axel Weber. One way to take account of real estate price developments would be to include owner-occupied housing in price indices. Since real estate prices have risen strongly in recent years, costs of owner-occupied housing are likely to have risen more strongly than average consumer prices.[5] This would be only a moderate modification, however. The best way for central banks to take into account price increases across a wider range of assets is probably within the second pillar of financial stability (Sect. 5.3).

[5] Rising real estate prices take time to translate into higher rents. Therefore, the difference in calculations with and without owner occupied housing is not as big as one might expect. The German Consumer Price Index (Preisindex der Lebenshaltung), for example, includes a pro-forma proxy for the rents of owner-occupied housing. Its rate of increase (1.6% in March 2018) is not significantly different from the Harmonized Consumer Price Index (HCPI) used by the ECB, which neglects owner occupied housing.

**4% Inflation or Price Level Targets?**

Despite the difficulties and the strong side-effects of today's narrow consumer price inflation targeting, some economists have recommended that central banks should try to push inflation rates to even higher levels. One idea has been to double inflation targets to 4%, another that central banks should use a price level target. This would imply that an undershooting of the inflation target during one period must be followed by an overshooting in the next. Proponents argue that, if central banks announced such policy changes, economic agents would expect future inflation rates to be higher. Therefore, financial markets would reach higher nominal interest rates, moving the economy away from the so-called zero lower bound. Central banks have been right not to follow such ideas, as they involve incalculable risks. First, a central bank's announcement alone cannot determine market expectations of price level changes. If central banks wanted to double inflation expectations, they would need to take further drastic action, such as even bigger asset purchases, negative central bank interest rates or pure money printing via helicopter money. As the transmission of monetary stimulus to demand and prices is highly uncertain, as shown in Chap. 3, one cannot be sure that even these radical measures would help to quickly reach the target. What is certain is that they would have exacerbated the unwanted side-effects of monetary accommodation for financial risk taking, the adequacy of retirement assets and the distribution of wealth. With the benefit of hindsight it is also clear that higher inflation targets, as discussed during the years of low inflation in 2015 and 2016, were not necessary to reflate economies. Rather, if even more forceful monetary stimuli had hit economies that were already growing strongly and approaching full employment, most notably the US and Germany, the result would have been even higher capacity utilization and cyclical overheating. In short: another boom certain to be followed by a bust.

## 5.2 Accounting for Trade-Offs with Financial Stability

> A narrative that attributes the decline in real rates primarily to an exogenous fall in the natural rate is incomplete. The influence of monetary and financial factors should not be ignored. …, an illustrative counterfactual experiment suggests that a monetary policy rule that takes financial developments systematically into account during both good and bad times could help dampen the financial cycle, leading to higher output even in the long run. Juselius et al. (2016, p. i)

"Inflation targeters" tend to take issue with the proposition that central banks should react in a systematic and symmetrical way to the risks of financial cycles. They primarily have doubts about two issues. First, how should central banks detect financial bubbles while they are emerging? Can they be smarter than (efficient) markets? Secondly, do central banks have the instruments and the power to effectively smooth financial cycles?[6]

Apart from theoretical discussions about market efficiency under real world assumptions, the assertion that markets are best at pricing risk is at odds with the massive short-term swings from underpricing to overpricing of risk frequently observed in financial cycles. Irrational behavior is all too common. The dot.com bubble in the late 1990s, with high-priced but loss-making companies and blind buying of IPOs, is but one good example.

A financial boom will typically be preceded by strong growth of money and credit aggregates. Hence, these indicators must be part of any attempt to systematically include financial cycles in monetary policy. Many additional indicators can be used to assess financial cycles, as collected and analyzed in the financial stability reports issued by central banks and international institutions as well as in their various financial condition indicators. Besides money and credit, indicators reflecting the valuation of stocks, bonds or real estate, volatility measures, lending standards and shadow banking indicators should be included in the analysis.

Judging by the IMF's index, financial conditions have been loose for a number of years and tightened only slightly since the Fed has begun decreasing the degree of accommodation in its policies (Fig. 5.2). The index also shows that financial conditions are typically very loose in advance of major market corrections, most notably in the run-up to 2008. Commenting on the situation in early 2018, IMF economists wrote: "Although still-easy financial conditions support economic growth in the near term, they may also contribute to a buildup of financial imbalances, excessive risk taking, and mispricing of risks. The growth-at-risk (GaR) approach—which links financial conditions to the distribution of future GDP growth outcomes—provides a framework for assessing the intertemporal trade-off between supporting growth in the near term and putting financial stability and future growth at risk over the medium term."[7]

The degree of accommodation or restriction that financial condition indicators show has to be assessed in the context of the overall economic environment. When growth is weak and economies show signs of slack, an attempt to loosen monetary and financial conditions is warranted.[8] After a long economic and financial upswing, however, loose monetary conditions create risks

---

[6] For a recent discussion of these issues see Lautenschläger (2018).

[7] IMF (2018, p. 1).

[8] Praet (2017).

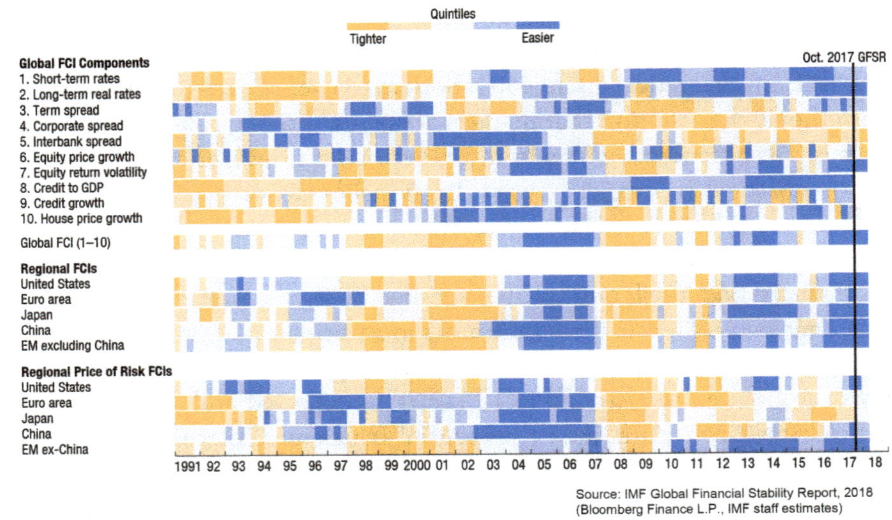


**Fig. 5.2** Global and regional FCIs and their components

for future growth, as the above quote enumerates.[9] In the late phases of a financial cycle, investors and financial institutes tend to become less risk averse, as their models produce benign signals due to high asset valuations, low volatility and low credit spreads. Very loose financial conditions then become a symptom of complacency, rather than stability.

This insight matters for monetary policy. As research by the BIS shows, attempts to smooth the financial cycle by leaning against the wind improve long-term economic performance. Technically, this is done by introducing a measure of financial conditions into the Taylor rule[10] for monetary policy and simulating output reactions. Of course, the Taylor rule is not a "ready to use blueprint" for monetary policy decisions,[11] and it is not directly applied as a decision rule by the ECB or other central banks; but it provides useful guidance to monetary policy. BIS researchers come to the conclusion that "an effective 'lean-against-the-wind' approach requires policy to take financial developments into account systematically. In effect, it may be represented by a policy rule that takes the form of an augmented version of the standard

[9] IMF (2018).

[10] The Taylor rule relates the central banks' interest rate to a long-term equilibrium rate, the output gap and the deviation of inflation from the target rate. It can be used as model explaining central banks rate setting behaviour.

[11] Praet (2017).

Taylor rule (Taylor 1993) and incorporates financial cycle indicators. …Using an illustrative policy rule that embodies such features, our analysis suggests that it would have been possible to mitigate financial imbalances, leading to significant output gains."[12]

The explicit inclusion of financial variables into the concept of monetary policy is more an issue of framing policy decisions rather than defining pre-determined reaction functions. The ECB takes financial indicators into consideration in its second policy pillar.[13] This so-called monetary pillar was intended to give long-term risks for price stability the necessary weight in policy decisions. Monetary aggregates and credit growth feature strongly among the variables included. Under the first pillar, meanwhile, the ECB defines the reference value for price stability and analyses reasons for possible deviations from this value. It was this first pillar that has predominantly shaped policy decisions in recent years. If the ECB gave the second pillar more weight, thus paying more attention to financial conditions,[14] it would not amount to a complete overhaul of its policy approach, merely a sensible rebalancing based on a broad set of financial cycle indicators.

There are doubts about whether the interest rate and other instruments of monetary policy are in fact powerful enough to stabilize markets in a period of boom and exuberance. Once speculative dynamics gain momentum, they are hard to break, as the discussion in Sect. 4.3 showes. On the other hand, central banks argue that low interest rates and large asset purchases can stimulate an economy. The flipside is that instruments of a more restrictive monetary policy should be able to dampen asset price inflation and risk-taking in periods of boom. "Pushing on a string" to stimulate economies should be more difficult than tightening the ropes in times of exuberance. The real issue is not whether central banks can influence the cycle in a boom, it is what the likely costs of such a strategy are. Short-term losses in terms of growth have to be weighed against long-run gains that ensue if financial bubbles are avoided

[12] Juselius et al. (2016, p. 3).

[13] Already in 2013 Ben Bernanke made the point for the Fed: "Financial stability is also linked to monetary policy, though these links are not yet fully understood. Here the Fed's evolving strategy is to make monitoring, supervision, and regulation the first line of defense against systemic risks; to the extent that risks remain, however, the Federal Open Market Committee strives to incorporate these risks in the cost–benefit analysis applied to all monetary policy actions" (Bernanke 2013, p. 12).

[14] The distinction between monetary and financial variables is not clear-cut. I prefer to speak of financial conditions as it has a broader connotation than monetary conditions, which may be associated more with control or target variables of monetary policy, such as interest rates, the yield curve or money and credit growth. Financial conditions would also encompass variables that indicate behavioral changes and sentiment changes on financial markets.

or at least mitigated. There is probably no conclusive answer to this question. Monetary authorities will need to use their judgement on a case-by-case basis.

## 5.3 The Role of More Discretionary Elements

Proponents of a simple policy rules may argue that a more flexible inflation target combined with more explicit consideration of financial indicators represents a step backwards towards discretionary policy making. So, why would more discretionary elements be a bad thing? They could be considered inevitable in view of deeply rooted uncertainties surrounding the effectiveness of monetary policy transmission and major structural shifts in the global economy in recent decades—such as unprecedented growth in global labor supply and the technologically-driven internationalization of supply chains that are affecting price determination. These profound changes have left central banks struggling to achieve their 2% target in recent years.

Hence the long-standing criticism that more discretionary monetary policies are time-inconsistent and generate an expansionary, i.e. inflationary bias seems to have lost some validity. The issue of time inconsistency is based on the view that only unexpected central bank actions create real effects on the economy. Therefore, central banks without binding policy rules may have an incentive to deviate from their stability targets in order to generate economic impact. In recent years, however, central banks have not been attempting to surprise markets by deviating from pre-announced targets, rather trying to reach them. With more room for discretionary decision-making, a central bank will hardly compromise on its commitment to price stability as long as this is its legal mandate. Risks for long-term price stability emanate from different sources, namely central banks increasingly becoming fiscal agents in an environment of quantitative easing policies (see Sect. 5.4).

In a two-pillar approach, which uses multiple indicators to guide policy decisions, there will be situations where conflicting signals of some indicators need to be resolved. One could, for example, imagine a late cycle environment after years of strong economic growth where inflationary pressures are high (signaling the need for tight monetary policy), while financial condition indicators, such as risk spreads, bank lending or money growth, are rapidly deteriorating (signaling the need for a loser policy stance). In such a situation, the central bank would have to figure out whether the deterioration of financial conditions signals a slowdown of activity that will eliminate unwanted inflationary pressures. If a central bank took this view, it should tolerate temporary overshooting of inflation and not tighten policy in a weakening financial environment.

Many other constellations are conceivable. If the ECB had taken financial market risks more explicitly into consideration, its policies would have been less expansionary since 2017. The euro area experienced its strongest growth in a decade and capacity utilization had returned to normal, while financial markets boomed and credit spreads plummeted.

With more room for discretionary policy decisions, a central bank can take into account trade-offs between price stability and financial risks as well as other trade-offs. The Fed, for example, pursues a more discretionary policy approach with its dual mandate "of stable prices and full employment". The Fed had to grapple with conflicting signals repeatedly in recent years. After the financial crisis, inflation initially stayed elevated despite weak economic activity. During those years, influential economists, including Larry Summers, Olivier Blanchard and Eugenio Cerutti, advocated that the Fed should focus less on inflation. They argued that inflation was not declining as strongly as the fall in output growth would suggest (a weak Phillips curve relationship), and that weak growth would have long-run effects on potential growth (hysteresis). They concluded that the Fed should have pursued more aggressive measures to stimulate the economy despite the slow decline in inflation.[15] In the years that followed, a different conundrum emerged as inflation stayed below a level considered as normal given the solid growth in GDP and employment. Conflicting signals from different indicators have neither harmed the Fed's transparency nor the consistency of its policies.

**Should the ECB Follow a Dual Mandate Like the Fed?**

Some economists recommend that the ECB should follow the Fed in adopting a dual mandate based on price stability and full employment. Such a mandate would provide the ECB with more room for discretionary decisions, for example in a situation where inflation is above target but full employment has not been achieved. The Fed can act more flexibly and give more weight to, for example, monthly labor market developments.

In this context, is important to note that the dual mandate of the Federal Reserve has evolved over time, mainly in the post WWII decades.[16] When the Fed was established in 1913 through the Federal Reserve Act, financial stability was its primary goal. Bouts of speculation and banking crises like the serious one of

(Continued)

[15] Blanchard et al. (2015).

[16] Bernanke (2013).

1907 had been in the focus of lawmakers. Inflation or price stability on the other hand had not been a major concern in the gold standard years and were not even mentioned as an explicit target for the central bank.[17] After the period of financial stabilization, which tragically failed in the Great Depression of the 1930s, came a period of fiscal dominance in which the Fed facilitated fiscal financing in varying degrees. It was not before the 1960s, after a long period of accommodation, that inflation began to rise and then surged with the oil price shocks of the 1970s. In those years price stability and macroeconomic stabilization took center stage. As other institutions were given more and more responsibility for financial regulation and supervision, the instruments deployed by monetary policy changed. Instead of reserves and margin requirements, for example, interest rates, open market operations and communication strategies became central instruments for the macro-management of the economy.

Nevertheless, a full-employment target seems inadvisable for the ECB. The ECB does not control the causes of unemployment, which vary widely between countries. Structural issues as well as wage and labor market policies in individual countries are critical for employment levels.[18] Thus a mandate to ensure full employment would overburden the ECB, particularly in a multi-country setting. National policy makers could blame the ECB for unemployment when it has been the result of misguided national policies.

Similar considerations would apply with regard to the strategy of nominal income targeting that has been a long-standing idea in monetary policy debates. In this concept, the central bank would aim at medium term growth of nominal incomes of say 5%. If growth is below that level, expansionary measures would be indicated, while higher figures would imply a dampening policy stance. The crucial question is, of course, whether such a target is reached through a combination of low real growth and high inflation or through high real growth and moderate inflation. As central banks do not have control, or even a strong influence, over real growth, they would be overburdened with the responsibility for reaching the aspired rate of inflation and real growth at the same time. Nominal income growth has, in former times, played an important role in the framework of money supply targeting that many central banks pursued in the eighties and early nineties. In such a framework, the amount of money supply can be derived from the medium term growth of nominal income, as long as there is a stable trend in money demand in the private sector. In this approach the central bank takes responsibility for reaching its intermediate target—money supply—but not for the growth of nominal income itself.

## 5.4 The Risks of QE as the New Normal

Attempts by the ECB and other major central banks to quickly reflate the economy in during the years of low inflation has led to a new era of policy making. Quantitative easing through large-scale purchases of government

[17] Reinhart and Rogoff (2013).

[18] For a more general discussion of the overburdening of central banks see Issing (2016).

bonds and other securities is now the new normal of monetary policy. Paradoxically, in the long run this new normal may prove much more inflationary than initially intended.

In June 2018, the ECB announced the end of its quantitative easing policy through large-scale asset purchases but a continuation of its zero interest rate policy until mid-2019, or as long as considered necessary. At that point, the euro area economy had enjoyed 10 years of economic growth, only interrupted by a patch of weakness during the debt crisis but accelerating again from 2016 onwards. The long period of accommodative monetary policy has stored up trouble. If the euro area entered an economic slowdown, or even a recession, in the near future, the ECB would hardly have any firepower left in terms of interest rate policy to stimulate the economy. It would probably have to resort to renewed asset purchases. Unconventional monetary policy would become part of the central bank's standard toolkit. The long-term implications of such a new normal in monetary policy are as yet unclear, but they are unlikely to be pretty.

The biggest concern is that, if the ECB continued to expand its balance sheet whenever the economy is weak, inflationary pressures would eventually emerge due to a massive surplus of central bank liquidity in the system. In recent years, the large amounts of liquidity have not stoked inflation as money and credit multipliers in the banking system were extremely weak. Once they normalize, however, and banks use abundant liquidity to extend credit to the economy, inflationary pressures will re-appear. The ECB would then attempt to quickly remove liquidity. Roughly, it would have two options to do that: First, it could start selling assets previously accumulated through QE or issue its own bonds to absorb liquidity. While technically simple, such measures would push up bond yields quite considerably in times of rising inflation. Government borrowing costs would rise and financial markets would be strained. Faced with such difficult trade-offs, the central bank might simply accept higher inflation.

The second option would be to neutralize the liquidity in the banking system by raising reserve requirements for banks. These requirements determine banks' ability to create money on their own. Higher reserve ratios would force banks to hold more central bank liquidity for a given volume of deposits. Their capacity to generate loans and money in the private sector would be reduced, monetary conditions would tighten and lending rates would be pushed up. In an extreme scenario, the ECB could set the reserve requirement at 100%, creating a system of full-reserve banking, replacing today's fractional reserve banking. The central bank would then control the money supply directly. Commercial banks would not be able to use deposits for lending;

they would have to acquire liquidity for lending purposes from the central bank, bond or equity markets. The central bank would be the main source of liquidity, responsible for supplying sufficient money and funds for the economy's financing needs. The banking system would no longer be able to adjust money supply in response to changes in money demand. If the central bank gets its liquidity policy wrong, it immediately creates either deflationary or inflationary pressures in the economy. Radical changes, like the introduction of full-reserve banking, are unlikely to occur. Unelected central bankers would become even more powerful than they are today, which would fuel political opposition. In Switzerland, a referendum rejected the introduction of full-reserve banking in June 2018.

Technically, the central bank may be able rein in or neutralize excessive liquidity in case inflation rises. They may, however, refrain from doing so because such moves would worsen government borrowing conditions. Having become the biggest holder of government bonds, any actions by the ECB have a strong fiscal impact. Therefore, political pressures on the ECB are likely to rise when it hikes interest rates or lowers government bond holdings to mop up some of the liquidity. The ECB's statutes as well as international law formally protects its independence. It is, however, not immune to public criticism. Demands to ease financial burdens for highly indebted countries in recent years have found recognition in the policies of quantitative easing. Finance ministers will surely also want to keep borrowing costs low in the future. A combination of low interest rates and some inflation is a way of easing the debt burden. Such policies, however, can undermine the objective of price stability pursued by the central bank.

It should not be overlooked that some economists and central bankers have started discussing even more radical forms of QE. The idea of "helicopter money" is that central banks buy perpetual government bonds that are never repaid or simply dispense additional cash and deposits to governments or households without taking in any assets at all. Such money creation, it is argued, would boost public demand without crowding out private demand through higher interest rates.

In an economy with a big shortfall of demand and a large amount of slack, helicopter money may have the intended impact. In an environment of almost full employment and positive output gaps, as has been the case in the US and many European economies recently, such a policy is bound to lead to inflation rather than growth of real demand and output.

Given the risks associated with a new normal of QE, central banks' best option would be to restore interest rates as the main tool of monetary policy. The US Fed opted to do so in 2015. Gradual tightening has not disrupted financial markets. Bond yields have risen without derailing strong growth in the US economy. In the meantime, the Fed has has started reducing its balance sheet. As the US has been ahead of the euro area in the current cycle, the Fed has had the opportunity to start normalizing monetary conditions at an earlier point of time than the ECB. Now the ECB should follow suit. The near-term risks of normalizing euro area interest rates seem manageable, while the long-term costs of not doing so appear considerable. If central banks are left with only balance sheet management in the next downturn, the consequences for inflation, central bank independence and economic stability might be dire.

## References

Bernanke BS (2013) A century of US central banking: goals, frameworks, accountability. J Econ Perspect 27(4):3–16

Bernanke BS, Laubach T, Mishkin FS, Posen AS (1999) Infaltion targeting—lessons from the international experience. Princeton University Press, Princeton

Blanchard O, Cerutti E, Summers L (2015) Inflation and activity—two explorations and their monetary policy implications (Working Paper No. 15/230). IMF

International Monetary Fund (2018) Global financial stability report, April 2018: a bumpy road ahead

Issing O (2016) Central banks—from overburdening to decline? (White Paper No. 42). SAFE, Goethe University

Issing O (2017) Financial stability and the ECB's monetary policy strategy. In: ECB legal conference 2017

Juselius M, Borio C, Disyatat P, Drehmann M (2016) Monetary policy, the financial cycle and ultra-low interest rates (Working Paper No. 569). Monetary and Economic Department, BIS.

Lautenschläger S (2018) Monetary policy—end of history? Speech presented at the Center for Financial Studies Colloquium in Frankfurt am Main, Germany

McKibbin WJ, Panton A (2018) 25 years of inflation targeting in Australia: are there better alternatives for the next 25 years? (Hutchins Center Working Paper Nr. 41)

Praet P (2017) Calibrating unconventional monetary policy. Speech presented at the ECB and its Watchers XVIII Conference organized by the Center for Financial Studies and the Institute for Monetary and Financial Stability at Goethe University in Frankfurt am Main, Germany, April 6

Reinhart CM, Rogoff KS (2013) Shifting mandates: the federal reserve's first centennial. Am Econ Rev 103(3):48–54

Tannenbaum CR (2018) A testing time for inflation targeting. Northern Trust

Taylor JB (1993) Discretion vs policy rules in practice. Carnegie-Rochester Conference Series on Public Policy 39

Weber A (2015) Rethinking inflation targeting. Project Syndicate

# 6

# Conclusions

*In the immediate aftermath of the global financial crisis, and in the case of the ECB, the European debt crisis, the central banks had to prevent dislocated financial markets from tipping their economies into a multiyear depression. While the central banks succeeded, political circumstances made it difficult to hand off the policy baton to other government agencies. As such, both the Fed and the ECB had little choice but to take on the bulk of the responsibility for bringing about better macroeconomic outcomes.*
Mohamed El-Erian, Bloomberg 12.6.2018 (See also El-Erian 2017)

The world's major central banks were the main actors in the crises of the past two decades. It was mainly up to them to take decisive action to prevent their economies from going into a tailspin. Their toolbox included drastic interest rate cuts and promises to keep interest rates low (forward guidance). Moreover, they assumed the role of lender of last resort for ailing banks and were involved in cases of recapitalization. While western central banks tackled the dot.com bubble in the early years of the century with conventional policy instruments, they entered uncharted territory with massive balance sheet expansion and partly negative interests after the Great Financial Crisis. The ECB, in particular, was not only confronted with weak growth in the euro area, but also potential disintegration of the currency union as markets speculated about the exit of some countries from the euro system. The ECB took drastic action in an attempt to stimulate growth and prevented the potential unravelling of the Euro currency union. It lowered its central rate to zero, pushed its deposit rate into negative territory, offered practically unlimited liquidity to banks and


M. Heise, *Inflation Targeting and Financial Stability*,
https://doi.org/10.1007/978-3-030-05078-8_6

ventured into large-scale bond purchases. Its promise to do "whatever it takes" to fend off speculation about denomination risks in the euro area finally calmed down markets. As a result of these measures, the ECB has not only become the lender of last resort for banks, a classical central bank function, but also the largest buyer of government bonds. It has more or less replaced the cross-border money market in the euro area, as all the liquidity needed for private cross-border transactions is provided by the European System of Central Banks, and imbalances in the flows between countries show up in the official payments system Target II. Also, sovereign bond prices are distorted by central bank intervention. The ECB influences the prices on sovereign bond markets mainly by its forward guidance on interest rate policies and by the bond purchasing program.

Although the Great Financial Crisis of 2008 was successfully resolved through the intervention of central banks, public expenditure programs, and the ECB's reassurance to markets that the European Currency Union was stable, growth and inflation in advanced economies continued to disappoint. Governments had to start reining in huge deficits and the instruments of central banks did not seem to have a strong impact on the economies. As households and the corporate sector needed to clean up their balance sheets and pay down some of the debt that had been accumulated in the boom, policies aimed at higher lending by financial institutions had only very limited impact. Consumers and companies did not behave in an interest sensitive way and much of the liquidity injected into the economy was parked as central bank deposits. For many years inflation rates stayed lower than central banks had promised. The ECB reacted by increasing the dose of its monetary stimulus. It was not before the year 2017, when commodity prices once again accelerated, that inflation came close to the bank's reference value of below, but close to 2%.

Given the profound changes in the global economy in recent years, the ability of monetary policy to steer GDP and inflation via its impact on national demand and capacity utilization is likely to have become much weaker. A most significant change has been the integration of an unprecedented number of workers from emerging Asia and former communist countries into the global economy. As global competition has intensified on goods and labor markets, the traditional patterns of wage and price formation seem to have been upturned. In many areas of manufacturing and the materials sector large excess capacity is putting pressure on prices. Competition is further intensified by the emergence of digital platforms that disrupt traditional business models, improve price transparency globally and empower consumers. Rapid advances in artificial intelligence and other digital technologies will continue to disrupt labor markets and price setting.

We do not yet fully understand what consequences such far-reaching global changes have for the workings of national economies. Therefore, economists and policy makers should be humble about their ability to foresee the effects of monetary policy on growth and inflation in this changing environment. Even with further research, uncertainty will remain.

In some areas, policy makers will even deal with radical or "Knightian" uncertainty, meaning that the probability distribution of events and their consequences cannot be known. The Great Financial Crisis is an example of such radical uncertainty, as it invalidated our understanding of the correlations that underpin financial markets. In future, political earthquakes such as Brexit or the threat of escalating trade wars and the uncertainty surrounding the impact of digital technologies on societies and economies will limit our ability to forecast.

Central bankers, too, operate in this environment of uncertainty. Our economies crucially depend on their judgements about the balance between intended but inherently uncertain effects of their monetary policies and possible unintended side-effects for growth and financial stability. While the objective of central banks remains the same—price stability in a broad sense—the means must be adapted to new uncertainties. Simple rules and reaction functions that take little account for side-effects will turn out to be costly, creating financial instability and lower long-term growth. A more flexible monetary policy framework—with an adaptable inflation target and explicit attention paid to the financial cycles—would allow central banks to take into account the uncertainties surrounding relevant economic causalities.

Despite the fact that we cannot easily trace and clearly quantify the effects of monetary policy on growth and inflation, governments have been relying on central banks to fix most problems in our economies. That is particularly true in the European Monetary Union, where ECB policies have been made responsible for many different objectives in recent years. However, a central bank cannot simultaneously achieve a combination of maintaining price stability and financial stability, fighting unemployment and keeping economies on track for higher growth, securing favorable borrowing conditions for our governments, stabilizing the Euro and regulating and supervising banks to avoid major risks. Reaching these goals requires action in various areas of policy, which has been rather neglected in many euro area countries. Fiscal policy had little room to support economic growth with extra spending or tax cuts, as the financial crisis had opened gaping deficits in public budgets. Consolidation was the name of the game in the years after 2009. It proceeded slowly, but it has, in the meantime, reduced average public deficits in the euro area to around half a percent of GDP in 2018. As fiscal policy had little room for maneuver, structural reforms in euro area countries aimed at better functioning goods and labor markets or more sustainable social security systems would have been all the more important. Central banks made it clear many times that they were "buying time" for fiscal consolidation and structural reforms to take place. While significant steps were taken in some member states, the overall pace of reform was moderate at best. Thus, a large part of the responsibility to improve economic outcomes was left with the central bank. The recent political trends towards populist and nationalist policies suggest that this will not materially change in the near future. Without much support through market-oriented, growth-friendly policies, the challenges for the ECB and other central banks will remain to be daunting. Political leadership is required to create the conditions necessary for competitiveness and growth of our economies. In the end, over-reliance on central banks will lead to secular weakness and less stability. Alas, central banks must not remain the only game in town.

## References

El-Erian M (2017) The only game in town: central banks, instability, and avoiding the next collapse. Random House Trade Paperbacks

El-Erian M (2018) What to expect from the Fed and the ECB this week. Bloomberg, June 12

# Appendix: Op-Ed List

## Project Syndicate

18. March 2018

### The Debt Shackles Return

By Michael Heise

*The only sustainable debt burden is one that can be managed even during cyclical downturns. Yet governments continue to repeat the same mistakes, treating debt as a boon for long-term growth, rather than what it is: a source of massive long-term risks.*

MUNICH—Global growth is accelerating. But before we break out the champagne, we should acknowledge the long-term risks to sustained expansion posed by rising private and public debt.

Market analysts view the uptick in private lending in most emerging and some developed economies as a sign of higher demand and a precursor of faster growth. But, while this is true in the short run, the relentless rise of overall debt remains among the most serious problems burdening the global economy.

Despite years of deleveraging after the 2008 global financial crisis, debt remains very high—and yet we have now returned to an expansionary credit cycle. According to the Bank for International Settlements, total non-financial


M. Heise, *Inflation Targeting and Financial Stability*,
https://doi.org/10.1007/978-3-030-05078-8

private and public debt amounts to almost 245% of global GDP, having risen from 210% before the financial crisis and around 190% at the end of 2001.

General government borrowing in the United States may reach 5% of GDP this year, pushing total public debt to about 108% of GDP. In the eurozone, public debt stands at about 85% of GDP; in Japan, the debt-to-GDP ratio registers close to an eye-popping 240%. Globally, private non-financial debt is growing faster than nominal GDP.

These trends are set to continue, as many major central banks—including the European Central Bank and the Bank of Japan—have not just welcomed the recovery in lending, but are even aiming to stimulate more credit-financed growth. Only the US Federal Reserve and the People's Bank of China are taking steps to rein in bank lending.

The world has endured enough economic crises to know that high debts create serious risks. Nominal debt is fixed, but asset prices can collapse, generating huge balance-sheet losses and causing risk premia—and thus borrowing costs—to rise. A mere decade ago, when a credit-fueled financial boom turned to bust, the financial sector was pushed to the brink of collapse, and a years-long recession followed in much of the world.

The only sustainable debt burden is one that can be managed even during cyclical downturns. Yet governments continue to repeat the same mistakes, treating debt as a boon for long-term growth, rather than what it is: a heavy burden and a source of massive long-term risks.

It is time for policymakers and their economic advisers to recognize this, and abandon the assumption that more debt always leads to more growth. Though there are times when governments need to borrow to stimulate the economy, deficit spending cannot lift growth in the long term. And at times when growth rates and private-sector borrowing are rising—times like now—governments should be working to reduce their own deficits. This is relevant for the US and Japan, but also for European Union countries, which should take advantage of today's recovery—the strongest in the decade—to bring their public finances in line with the Stability and Growth Pact.

Governments should seek to prevent the buildup of unsustainable debt by stimulating long-term, non-debt-financed growth, using a combination of regulation, trade agreements, investment incentives, and educational and labor-market reforms. In a low-inflation environment like the one prevailing today, central banks can cushion the impact of such reforms through expansionary monetary policies.

But central banks must calibrate their interventions carefully, to ensure that monetary expansion does not encourage the buildup of even more private-sector leverage. This means thinking twice before enforcing negative deposit rates, designed to pressure banks to lend more, or liquidity operations conditioned on bank lending.

A better approach would emphasize the use of forward guidance to influence interest-rate expectations and bond yields. Low yields can fuel asset-price increases and stimulate demand in a range of areas, not only through higher corporate leverage. That said, with asset prices already high and economies growing at a healthy pace, central banks should follow the Fed's lead in gradually unwinding the stimulus programs they initiated after the 2008 crisis.

Moreover, regulators should do more to ensure that private debt is channeled toward productive uses offering decent longer-term returns. This is the lesson from previous debt crises, including the subprime mortgage bubble that triggered the meltdown a decade ago, with devastating consequences for growth and employment.

For example, regulatory authorities can employ macroprudential policies to impose limits on segments of financial markets that are overheating, thereby improving the allocation of capital and stabilizing investment returns. They should take particular care to prevent real-estate bubbles, because real estate constitutes a huge share of overall wealth and a key source of collateral in finance. But the strong rise of low quality leveraged loans should also be a concern.

None of this will be easy for governments, regulators, or central banks. Monetary tightening may slow growth temporarily; preventing the growth of bubbles is notoriously difficult; and the types of structural reforms needed to secure a shift away from debt-fueled growth are hardly ever popular. Today's febrile political environment certainly will not simplify matters.

But the consequences of shying away from such choices could be devastating. The financial cycle will continue to gain momentum, eventually causing asset prices to overshoot fundamentals by a wide margin; leverage ratios will rise even further, and demand will outstrip capacity, spurring inflation.

At that point, an external shock or a decision by central banks to apply the monetary brakes—an inevitable response to mounting exuberance and rising inflation—will lead to a potentially ruinous crash. Financial markets, hopped up on low interest rates and ample liquidity, would take a major hit. Private leverage and public debt levels would suddenly look a lot less sustainable.

Times may be good, but good times are precisely when risks build up. Policymakers cannot say they have not been warned.

## Financial Times

13. December 2017

### Fed's failure to tighten financial conditions a cause for concern

By Michael Heise

The Federal Reserve has raised interest rates three times since the end of 2016, and in September announced a reduction of its $4.5tn balance sheet. Despite the Fed's gradual removal of monetary accommodation, monetary conditions have not tightened—they have become looser. Corporate credit spreads have declined, long-term interest rates have hardly changed, stock markets keep going up and the dollar has not appreciated markedly. What explains this apparent paradox? There are three possible reasons.

The first is that investors simply do not believe that the Fed is serious. After years of ultraloose monetary policy, they are convinced that the central bank will not risk any big setbacks in financial markets. They expect tightening to be very cautious and thus remain sanguine about buoyant asset prices. The Fed, however, is consistent in its forward guidance towards higher rates and has so far in 2017 done what it had promised. Investor optimism, therefore, is unlikely to explain the dearth of market reaction—and it certainly cannot explain why monetary conditions have actually eased. A second possible reason is that the healthy global economy has boosted equity and corporate bond markets, and this impact has outweighed that of monetary tightening. Higher growth, however, should also lead to rising long-term bond yields, something that has not materialised. Ten-year Treasuries have remained more or less flat since December last year.

The most plausible explanation for the monetary policy paradox is found in the global financial context. Not only the Fed, but also the European Central Bank and the Bank of Japan have an impact on the prices for global fixed-income assets. As long as they stick to a course of extreme monetary accommodation and keep interest rates on European and Japanese government bonds ultra-low, especially on the long end, the Fed's tightening will have limited impact on longer-term Treasuries. It will mainly flatten the yield curve, as we have seen in recent months.

The background is that bond yields in the euro area and Japan have become more important for global developments in recent years. The supply of safe assets has declined after the global financial crisis, while investor demand has risen. Eurozone benchmark bonds and Japanese government bonds have, to some extent, become substitutes for Treasuries as safe assets. Their prices, therefore, impact on Treasury prices. Empirical analysis substantiates this argument. The same, by the way, does not (yet) hold for China. The recent strong rise in Chinese bond yields has had no noticeable impact on global bond markets. Despite China's global economic importance, its government bonds are not seen as safe assets. Chinese monetary policies, recently geared towards slowing credit growth, seem to have a direct impact mainly on national bond yields.

The linkages between markets for safe assets, meanwhile, create difficult choices for policymakers. Since neither the ECB nor the BoJ look set to tighten measurably in the near future, the Fed's conundrum will endure. US financial conditions will stay lose even as the Fed tightens. This creates risk. The International Monetary Fund in its latest stability report reminded us that risks to financial stability and growth always build up in good times. Continued favourable financing conditions and soaring asset prices breed complacency and excessive risk-taking.

What are the plausible scenarios going forward? The fact that the ECB and the BoJ are behind the curve may force the Fed to take more hawkish steps than markets expect. This would strengthen the US dollar and widen the already large yield gap between Treasuries and German or Japanese government bonds. Financial markets would be caught off guard and prices of risk assets would tumble. As the Fed is aiming for gradual policy tightening, this scenario does not look very likely. The US tax reform is not expected to have a big impact on growth that would put pressure on the Fed.

An alternative scenario is that the ECB and the BoJ start tightening more vigorously than expected. This would also shake up global markets, which are counting on a long period of accommodation in these regions. Fundamentals might point in the direction of some monetary tightening at least in Europe, as growth is solid and capacity well utilised. But given current forward guidance of both the ECB and the BoJ, a more vigorous tightening in 2018 or 2019 seems very unlikely.

This leaves a rather bullish scenario for global markets. The impact of the Fed's tightening will remain limited, while a change of heart at the ECB and the BoJ looks unlikely. Other factors may spook markets, including geopolitical risks, higher oil prices or trade protectionism. But monetary policies are unlikely to be disruptive as long as inflation remains subdued, which seems likely. The result? Financial risk will continue to build up and market overheating becomes more likely. Investors will have to carefully navigate this paradox financial cycle if they want to avoid being caught off guard.

## Financial Times

26 September 2017

### Bond markets need to wake up to global upswing

*by Michael Heise*

Since the financial crisis in 2008, the global economy has been characterised by slow growth, low inflation and extremely expansionary monetary policies. Markets seem to expect a continuation of this so-called "new normal". They predict no interest rate rises in the foreseeable future from either the ECB or the Bank of Japan, and they expect the Fed funds rate to stay lower than indicated by the Fed's governors.

After years of sluggish growth, many people seem to be stuck in a "great recession" or secular stagnation mindset. There are, however, clear signs of a cyclical recovery and it is accelerating.

First, global trade is staging a comeback—notwithstanding the protectionist rhetoric of some political leaders. After two dismal years in 2015 and 2016, the trade recovery is fuelled by a recovery in the Chinese economy and the turn of commodity markets. The interlinkages of trade are reinforcing global growth.

Second, globally, a new expansionary credit cycle is supporting growth. In emerging Asia, credit growth remains strong, despite policy efforts to limit financial stability risk, especially in China. In the US, the credit cycle turned about three years ago, with first the corporate sector and then households assuming more debt. The debt-to-GDP ratio in the private non-financial sector, which had declined massively in the years following the financial crisis, has been rising again since 2014. In the eurozone, the new credit cycle is in its infancy, but here, too, loans to the private sector are rising again. The time of deleveraging and consolidation of private debt is over.

Finally, capacity utilisation in most developed markets is back to normal or even above normal. Current estimates of output gaps indicate there is hardly any slack in the world's big economies. That is true even in the eurozone, where capacity utilisation in manufacturing is reported to be above average. While it is true that prices and wages and prices in today's globalised and digitised economy don't react to capacity utilisation as strongly as they used to in former decades, it seems unrealistic to expect no reaction at all. Improving business confidence, little idle capacity and tightening labour markets will at least gradually increase wage demands and output prices.

What does the economic upswing imply for bond yields and stock markets? Usually, we would expect bond yields to be roughly in line with nominal GDP, both on the basis of economic logic and historical experience. But while nominal GDP growth has averaged 2.7 per cent in the eurozone and 3.5 per cent in Germany in the last three years, bond yields have remained much lower, in many countries close to zero.

One reason for this discrepancy is, of course, monetary policy. Our own estimates, as well as statements by ECB officials, suggest that the central bank's asset purchase programme has pushed down the German 10-year Bund yield by about 0.8 percentage points. A normalisation of monetary policies, notably an end to QE, would drive up bond yields. By how much is an open question, as the phasing out of QE will to some extent have been priced into yields already. An exit, if done carefully and gradually, should therefore not unsettle markets. It would leave eurozone bond yields much below nominal growth rates.

Bond yields could react more forcefully, if and when market participants upgrade their expectations concerning future growth and inflation. Once investors wake up to the return of the economic cycle, their expectations about interest rates and the course of monetary policy will also change. The ECB is cautioning against overly optimistic expectations and remains expansionary in its forward guidance. But as the cyclical expansion gains force, central banks might have to take tougher action to correct an excessively expansionary path. Further delaying the exit from QE therefore harbours risks.

Rising bond yields in an economic expansion are nothing unusual and should not cause a fundamental repricing of stocks. After all, even bond yields of 2 or 3 per cent imply price earnings ratios for bonds that are way above stock market valuations. The transition from a "new normal" with a rather bleak outlook to a more cyclically driven expansion will inevitably generate volatility. Keeping it low as low as possible is a challenge for the ECB. A timely, but gradual correction of monetary policy is the best option.

## Project Syndicate

2. March 2017

### Rewriting the Monetary-Policy Script

By Michael Heise

*Many central bankers, intoxicated by rigid neo-Keynesian models of the effects of interest rates on demand and inflation, are ignoring a major lesson from decades of experimentation: the impact of monetary policy cannot be predicted with a high degree of certainty or accuracy. To manage risk, flexibility is key.*

MUNICH—How long will major central banks blindly rely on rigid rules to control inflation and stimulate growth? Given the clear benefits of nimble monetary policy, central bankers need to open their eyes to the possibilities that flexibility affords.

The rule of thumb for monetary policymakers has long been that if inflation is below official target ranges, short-term interest rates should be set at a level that spurs spending and investment. This approach has meant that once interest rates reach or approach zero, central banks have little choice but to activate large asset-purchase programs that are supposed to stimulate demand. When circumstances call for it, policymakers default to the predetermined scripts of neo-Keynesian economic models.

But in too many cases, those scripts have led us astray, because they assume that monetary policy has a measurable and foreseeable impact on demand and inflation. There is plenty of reason to question this assumption.

For starters, households have not responded to ultra-low interest rates by saving less and spending more. If savings no longer yield a return, people can't afford big-ticket items or pay for retirement down the road. Likewise, companies today are faced with so much uncertainty and so many risks that ever-lower costs of capital have not enticed them to invest more.

It's easy to see why, despite the data, predetermined formulas are attractive to monetary policymakers. The prevailing wisdom holds that in order to return the inflation rate to a preferred level, any slack in the economy must be eliminated. This requires pushing interest rates as low as possible, and when these policies have run their course (such as when rates dip toward the negative), unconventional instruments like "quantitative easing" must be deployed to revive growth and inflation. The paradigm has become so universally accepted—and the model simulations underpinning central banks' decisions have become so complex—that few are willing to question it. For individual central banks or economists, to do so would be sacrilege.

Central banks do not completely deny the economic costs that these policies imply: exuberance in financial markets, financing gaps in funded pension systems, and deeper wealth inequality, to name just a few. But these costs are deemed an acceptable price to pay to reach the clearly defined inflation level.

Yet the policies pursued in recent years have given no room for the intangibles—unstable political environments, geopolitical tremors, or rising risks on financial markets—that can send models off course. As the 2008 financial crisis illustrated, the normal distribution of risk was useless for predictions.

Keynes never tired of arguing that monetary policy becomes ineffective if uncertainty is sufficient to destabilize the expectations of consumers and investors. Unfortunately, many central banks have forgotten this. The Bank of Japan, the Bank of England, and the European Central Bank all hone to rather rigid policy rules. If expansionary policies fail to have the desired effect of lifting inflation to the predefined level of around 2%, they do not question their models; they simply increase the policy dosage—which is just what markets expect.

For now, the US Federal Reserve has the most flexible toolkit among the major central banks. In addition to inflationary pressure, the Fed's monetary policy must also take into account employment statistics, growth data, and the stability of financial markets. But even the Fed's flexibility is under siege. Republican lawmakers are discussing how to bind the Fed to more scripted policy rules to manage inflation (using a formula known as the Taylor rule, which predetermines changes in the federal funds rate in relation to inflation and an output gap). Needless to say, such a move would be a mistake.

Central banks (not to mention lawmakers), with their strong attachment to neo-Keynesian theory, are ignoring a major lesson from decades of monetary-policy experimentation: the impact of monetary policy cannot be predicted with a high degree of certainty or accuracy. But the belief that it can is essential to the credibility of the now-standard inflation targets. If central banks keep missing these rather narrow marks ("below, but close to 2%"), they end up in an expectations trap, whereby markets expect them to dispense ever higher doses of monetary medicine in a frantic attempt to reach their target.

Clearly, such monetary policies create soaring costs and risks for the economy. And central banks themselves are coming dangerously close to looking like fiscal agents, which could undermine their legitimacy.

A new and more realistic monetary paradigm would discard overly rigid rules that embody the fallacy that monetary policy is always effective. It would give central banks more room to incorporate the risks and costs of monetary policies. With such a paradigm, central banks could move away from negative interest rates and large-scale asset purchases. They would define their inflation targets more flexibly, to avoid being forced into action whenever "uncertainties" such as declining oil prices or required wage adjustments cause inflation to move above or below 2%.

Perhaps most important, a new paradigm would acknowledge the limits of central banks' power and foresight. That would remove an alibi that governments too often hide behind to avoid introducing the structural reforms that really matter for long-term growth.

## Financial Times

August 21, 2016

### Monetary policy lacks the muscle to boost growth

The answer must be to strengthen our economies' potential to create jobs, writes **Michael Heise**

In Japan, Prime Minister Shinzo Abe announces yet another fiscal stimulus. In Europe, economists nod approvingly when the euro group waives fines on Spain—which, despite years of growth, still runs deficits way higher than the bloc's rules allow. In the US, both presidential candidates promise more government spending.

So it is clear that attempts, however tentative, to cut spending and pay down debt have given way to renewed enthusiasm for policies such as these, that are intended to boost demand instead. This is dangerous. If governments resort to sky-high debt and negative interest rates, despite moderate growth and normalised capacity utilisation, in an upswing, what will they do if and when their economies weaken again?

Especially in Europe and Japan, policymakers have been trying relentlessly to generate growth through bank lending and fiscal borrowing. The Bank of Japan and the European Central Bank have turned interest rates negative to punish banks that fail to convert their cash reserves into loans.

At the same time, these central banks are buying huge amounts of government and corporate bonds. The resulting low, or negative, interest rates help governments to continue running large deficits. Many economists support such policies: if the private sector does not borrow, they argue, then the public sector must do so to generate demand.

Not surprisingly, however, expansionary monetary policies have done little to fuel bank lending and private-sector borrowing. Reviving lending after a financial crisis is like pushing on a string: central banks can smooth out the inevitable debt reduction process by cutting interest rates and pumping liquidity into the banking system; but they cannot totally eliminate the need for companies, banks and households to pay down excessive debt. It usually takes years; this time is no different.

Given that monetary policy lacks muscle, many argue that public deficit spending must compensate for the lack of private demand. Governments should borrow more to invest in infrastructure and innovation. These recommendations are aimed especially at countries such as Germany that have balanced their budgets. But critics of "misguided austerity" are vocal in France and other, southern European nations, too. In their view, the eurozone's caps on public deficits and debt have only made the crisis worse.

This story is simply not supported by facts. Debt levels have continued to rise since the financial crisis in most developed countries. In both the US and the eurozone, total nonfinancial sector debt (public and private) increased from about 225 per cent of gross domestic product in 2007 to 250 per cent in 2015. Most of this was in the public sector. If growing debt could fuel growth, we would be fine.

We are not. More debt clearly is not the solution to the west's growth problem. The answer must be to strengthen our economies' potential to create more and better jobs. Sure, structural reforms feature among the recommendations of the International Monetary Fund, the OECD and many central banks. Back in the real world, policymakers focus almost exclusively on policies to boost demand.

Many economists who support this view argue that structural reforms work only in the long run. In the short term, they may even be counterproductive because they widen the gap between supply and demand in an economy.

Some look askance at structural reforms, too, claiming they improve the competitiveness and export performance of one economy only at the expense of its trading partners. This is muddled thinking. Policy measures that improve productivity and innovation are good for growth irrespective of how open an economy is.

The lesson we should have learnt from the post-crisis years is that demand-boosting policies on their own cannot return our economies to sustainable growth. Monetary policies are not very effective. Fiscal policies can certainly help—but only if they trigger investment and innovation and enable structural reforms.

But this is not what happened. While total government debt in the eurozone jumped by about €3tn between 2007 and 2015, public investment spending actually fell by about €20bn. Meanwhile, structural reforms came to be considered a nice-to-have rather than the foundation of sustainable growth.

Greater innovation and higher productivity remain the safest routes to restored growth and wealth generation. And this needs open markets, tax incentives for investment and a wellqualified workforce—not ever more fiscal spending and central bank cash injections. *The writer is chief economist of Allianz.*

## Wall Street Journal

### Hitting the Limits of Monetary Policy

*Even ECB President Mario Draghi admits he's running out of options.*

By Michael Heise
March 17, 2016

Last week, the European Central Bank announced its latest round of interest-rate cuts and a further expansion of its already sizable asset-purchase program, known as quantitative easing. This came barely three months after the ECB already had extended QE and cut its deposit rate back in December, an indication that such tactics are having a diminishing effect on the economy. ECB President Mario Draghi has signaled that we've perhaps reached the limits of what monetary policy can do to help the European Union reach its target of 2% inflation.

This should come as no surprise. Interest rates at zero or below, combined with an expanded central-bank balance sheet through QE, has been a strategy employed by central banks in the eurozone, U.K., Japan and the U.S. to increase liquidity and raise both market expectations of inflation as well as actual inflation. But so far, the new monetary-policy paradigm hasn't had the desired effect on these economies. Inflation and inflation expectations around the world today are much lower than central banks would like.

The prevailing doctrine is that the real interest rate, which is the difference between the observed interest rate and the rate of inflation, needs to be reduced to the point where it establishes an economic equilibrium with full employment. Since central banks can push headline rates into negative territory only to a limited extent, they also need to stoke inflation through unconventional measures like QE. Eventually, consumption and investment activity should pick up, and more jobs should be created, until full employment is restored. Or so the theory goes.

But success is by no means guaranteed. Economics textbooks pinpoint various situations in which monetary policy can fail to work. Even John Maynard Keynes, the father of modern anticyclical-demand management, highlighted certain conditions that could render monetary policy ineffective. As he pointed out, a central bank can expand the money supply all it likes, but if the funds are simply hoarded in the banking system or by households, economic activity doesn't accelerate.

Besides this so-called liquidity trap, monetary policy can also become ineffective when companies fail to increase their capital spending in response to falling interest rates and growing liquidity. Economic uncertainty can lead to an investment trap in which investors adopt a wait-and-see approach.

What's important to understand is that the transmission of monetary stimulus into real economic activity isn't based on stable and reliable economic relationships. Low interest rates and a generous supply of liquidity drive up the prices of assets such as equities, bonds and real estate. But these gains can only be sustained if the real economy improves at the same time. Otherwise a liquidity boom on stock markets can quickly implode again.

This is what happened at the beginning of this year, when negative news about the Chinese and U.S. economies caused a crash on global stock markets. If consumers don't spend more as a result of rising asset valuations and low interest rates, the impact of monetary policy is at best a temporary boost to financial prices. Meanwhile, as low returns fuel fears that retirement provisions may prove inadequate, many people may be inclined to save more, further impeding spending.

Loose monetary policy also depends on the credit channel. If businesses and households are reluctant to borrow more, the impact of monetary policy will be muted. The additional liquidity created by QE will remain in the banking system instead of flowing into the real economy.

Subdued credit growth is typical following a financial crisis, including the one in 2008, which in many countries exposed excessive private-sector debt levels. A prolonged period of deleveraging tends to follow, as corporations, banks and households repair their balance sheets. This phase, known as a balance-sheet recession, also renders monetary policy much less effective.

Under such conditions, negative interest rates or additional liquidity injections won't restore full employment. Other policy instruments are needed, such as an increase in productivityenhancing government infrastructure spending, tax incentives to boost business investment, and improved regulation and liberalization of markets to help job creation. After years of monetary easing, it's obvious that attention must now shift to such policies. Central bankers, including Mr. Draghi, have rightly been calling for more support on this side.

Monetary-policy strategies still need to be rethought. The cracks in its transmission mechanisms are glaringly obvious, and explain why such programs haven't achieved their objectives. Simply increasing the dose of an ineffective medicine risks exacerbating its undesirable side effects. In this case, long-term saving plans suffer, funded pension systems come under pressure, investors take on higher risks, money markets no longer work and financial markets become hypersensitive to tweaks in interest rates.

Central banks don't have the power to control growth and inflation at all times. If the advanced economies want to achieve a stable equilibrium with full employment, they need other economic policies. Too much has been left to central banks to sort out. It is time for burden-sharing.

Mr. Heise is the chief economist at Allianz SE.

Link:

http://www.wsj.com/articles/hitting-the-limits-of-monetary-policy-1458236689

## Financial Times: Markets Insight

**17 Feb 2016**

### Don't forget the upside of 'lower for longer' oil

*It's time to remember the fundamentals—low oil prices will boost the global economy*

by Michael Heise

For weeks, markets have been mirroring the oil price. Investors consider slumping oil prices as evidence of lacklustre global demand. They are not convinced lower energy costs can lift global demand, as they have done in the past. It is time to go back to fundamentals. Lower oil prices will deliver a boost to the global economy. This time is not different.

Countries that are net importers of oil make up the bulk of the world economy. For them, lower oil prices translate into higher real incomes, which should increase private consumption. Of course, falling oil prices have drastically reduced earnings of oil producers, who have since been forced to slash investment spending. Also, aggregate demand in oil-exporting countries is declining—albeit not in proportion to falling oil revenues, as governments use their cash reserves to smooth the downturn.

Such economic effects were also visible in the mid-1980s, when Opec's attempts to gain market share brought the oil price crashing to $10 per barrel. It took some time for the price collapse to work through the system. Eventually growth accelerated to varying degrees in virtually all industrialised countries between 1987 and 1990.

The demand stimulus from lower oil prices is usually reinforced by a positive supply shock—a mechanism that economists like Michael Bruno and Jeffrey Sachs proved back in the 1980s. These supply-side effects are not immediate. It takes time before lower production costs affect prices and production plans.

I cannot see why these laws of economics should be defunct in 2016. True, the fiscal surpluses in oil-producing countries have been eroded after years of lavish public spending. Oil producers have, however, also built up huge sovereign wealth funds. Most of these funds are replete enough for governments to cushion the economic blow of low prices, at least for a while.

I would also expect the supply-side effects to kick in due course. The use of oil in global production has decreased since the mid-1980s, especially in rich countries that have shifted to less energy-intensive manufacturing and services. At the same time, however, there has been a massive build-up of production capacity in emerging markets, which is often rather energy-intensive. China's net oil imports amount to 2 per cent of GDP. In Taiwan the figure is 7 per cent, with most of the other emerging Asian countries somewhere in between. Their economies will benefit from lower import prices.

Overall, the direct economic impact of cheaper oil may be somewhat weaker than in previous cycles. But this time around, central banks have been reacting forcefully to the perceived deflationary threats of lower oil prices. Expansionary monetary policies are reinforcing the positive demand and supply effects.

I reckon that the global growth impact of falling oil prices in 2014 and 2015 will be at least three-quarters of a percentage point. Part of this effect has already taken place and has helped to mitigate other strong headwinds for growth, especially in emerging markets. But the larger part is still to come.

Another long-term impact of low oil prices will be seen on capital markets. With lower oil revenues, the savings glut in oil-producing countries is about to disappear, and the global supply of capital will decline. At the same time, many emerging markets, above all China, are shifting their growth models towards consumption and away from savings and investment. Over time, these shifts in the supply of capital should push up rates of return globally—a welcome step back towards normality.

The key question for me, therefore, is not whether the laws of economics are defunct, but whether the oil price will stay low (say in the $25–50 range) for long enough for these laws to be set in motion. Under current circumstances, this looks likely.

Forecasting oil prices remains fiendishly difficult. Only a couple of years ago, many respected analysts predicted oil supply to peak and the oil price to stay extraordinarily high as a result. That turned out to be wrong. Not only supply and demand determine the oil price but also new technologies, financial market speculation, geopolitical tensions and the not always transparent political objectives of large producer countries.

So for us economists, the safest way to ponder the impact of oil prices is through scenarios based on different price assumptions. If you assume that the oil price stays lower for longer, expect good news for economic growth and financial markets.

*Michael Heise is chief economist of Allianz SE.*

Link to article:

http://www.ft.com/intl/cms/s/0/23e3a466-cf32-11e5-92a1-c5e23ef99c77.html#axzz40Q19hi8E